Stadium Stories:

New England Patriots

Jim Donaldson

INSIDERS' GUIDE®

GUILFORD, CONNECTICUT
AN IMPRINT OF THE GLOBE PEQUOT PRESS

INSIDERS' GUIDE®

Text design: Casey Shain

Cover photos: *front cover*: Adam Vinatieri (AP/Wide World). *Back cover*: top, Gino Cappelletti (AP/Wide World); bottom, Bill Belichick (Joe Robbins).

Library of Congress Cataloging-in-Publication Data
Donaldson, Jim.
    Stadium stories : New England Patriots / Jim Donaldson. — 1st ed.
      p. cm. — (Stadium stories series)
    ISBN 0-7627-3788-3
      1. New England Patriots (Football team)—History. I. Title. II. Series.

GV956.N36D66 2005
796.332'64'0974461—dc22   2005047642

Manufactured in the United States of America
First Edition/First Printing

This one's for the boys—James and Ben, fortunate young sports fans who not only have seen the Patriots win three Super Bowls in four years but also saw the Red Sox win a World Series.

Contents

Acknowledgments

These aren't my Patriots stadium stories. I just wrote them down after listening to them told eloquently and amusingly by such terrific—and fascinating—guys as Gino Cappelletti, who is in the Patriots Hall of Fame and, as one of the greats of the old AFL, deserves a spot in the Pro Football Hall of Fame; his long-time broadcast partner, Gil Santos; my dear friend Ron Hobson, who has covered the Patriots every year of the team's existence and, since I began covering the team in 1979, has provided me with countless laughs and good times; and former Patriots such as Pete Brock, Steve Nelson, and Bob "Harpo" Gladieux. I thank all of them profusely, along with Stacey James, the hardworking director of media relations for the Patriots; and Jim Gigliotti, whose editorial expertise, encouragement, suggestions, and support are greatly appreciated.

No Place Like Home

Where there's smoke, there's . . . well, yeah . . .
fire. "It was on our side of the field," said the
Patriots long-time play-by-play man Gil Santos, recalling the blaze in the stands at
Alumni Stadium at Boston College when he
was broadcasting a preseason game against
the Falcons in 1969. "The radio booth at BC
was right on top of the stands, which at that
time were wooden bleachers. I saw people

down below me, off to my right, starting to scatter away from one area. Then I saw smoke, followed by a mad dash of fans running down, out of the bleachers, right onto the field. Smoke was billowing up. Flames were shooting up. The referee stopped the game. Our booth was wooden, so I'm thinking, 'If the stands are on fire, there's a good chance this booth will catch fire, too.' We're figuring we'd better get out of there."

Ever the professional, however, Santos remained cool on the air as the heat rose from the burning bleachers, continuing to speak in that deep, basso profundo voice so familiar to generations of Patriots fans in New England. While Santos was describing to listeners what was happening, he had his producer call the radio station to alert the people back at the studio that he was about to go off the air.

"At that time," Santos said, "one of our sponsors was Narragansett Beer. They had a series of television commercials in which the punch line was, 'But first, I'll have one more Gansett.' Just before I'm about to send it back to the station, as I'm describing how the flames are shooting up, and the stands are burning, and that we're about to go off the air, I say, 'But first, I'll have one more Gansett.'

"As it turned out, we never did leave the booth. The firemen arrived on the scene very quickly, and it didn't take them long to put the fire out. We stayed in the booth and watched them."

It later was learned that the cause of the fire was a popcorn machine at a concession stand under the wooden bleachers. Somehow the oil began to blaze, and the flames were swept upward by the air moving through the openings in the stands. "Fortunately nobody got hurt," Santos said. "And it wasn't a huge section of seats that were burned. After the fire was out, everybody found a seat, and the game continued. Popcorn sales, of course, were down."

It was no laughing matter while the smoke was roiling. Afterward, however, it was easy to see humor in the situation. "It was funny," Santos said, "to see the fans out on the field, hobnobbing with the players. They were all standing around together, talking, and watching the fire."

Gino Cappelletti, who for the past twenty-four years has been the color analyst on the Patriots radio broadcasts, then was one of the team's star players. He was the team's top pass catcher, as well as the placekicker. "We didn't know what was happening," Cappelletti said, "until fans started to come onto the field. Then we saw the smoke and flames in the stands. We were standing around on the field, and fans started coming up to us, putting their arms around our shoulder pads. They were talking to the Atlanta guys, too. Everybody was asking: 'Hey, how you doin'? What town are you from? Isn't this something?'"

There was always something that seemed to be in the way of the Patriots finding a permanent place to play. Of course, given the history of pro football in Boston, the idea of permanency seemed a pipe dream for Billy Sullivan's fledgling American Football League franchise when it opened the 1960 season on Friday night, September 9, against the Denver Broncos at Boston University Field.

Before the Patriots came to town, they had been preceded in Boston by the Bulldogs, Bears, Shamrocks, Yanks (is it any wonder a team with that nickname failed to survive in Boston?), and in 1932 an NFL team called the Braves, owned by George Preston Marshall, which played at the home of the city's National League baseball team, Braves Field. When the baseball Braves raised the rent, Marshall moved to nearby Fenway Park where the Red Sox played, and renamed his team the Redskins. They lasted in Boston until 1937, when Marshall abandoned the city in favor of Washington.

Even though Boston had been the largest city in the country—and the largest television market—without a pro football team, there was no reason to think the Patriots would last any longer than previous teams.

Boston University Field was a scaled-down version of the former Braves Field, where Sullivan had been public-relations man for the Braves in the glory days of Warren Spahn and Johnny Sain. Spahn and Sain pitched the team to the pennant in 1948, when the watchword in Boston no longer was "One if by land, and two if by sea," but "Spahn and Sain, and two days of rain."

The Patriots spent three years there, but seating was limited to just over 20,000, and parking was a problem. So in 1963 the team moved to Fenway Park. "Of all the places we played, that was my favorite," said Cappelletti, who played for the Patriots from their inception through 1970, the season before they moved to Foxboro. "Fenway Park," Cappelletti said, "gave us the feeling of being truly professional. We dressed in the Red Sox locker room, where Ted Williams and so many other great players had been. And when we went out on the field, it was like being in the heart of Boston. It meant a lot to us."

The Patriots played there, with one exception, through the 1968 season. That was the year that, because of a conflict with the Red Sox, the Pats had to play their "home" opener in Birmingham, Alabama. The folks in Birmingham were hoping Sullivan and the Patriots might move south permanently. By then Billy had been lobbying for nearly a decade to get a stadium built in Boston for his team, but he was no closer to achieving his goal than he had been when he acquired the franchise in 1959.

Other cities were interested in acquiring the Patriots as well—Jacksonville, Memphis, Seattle, and Tampa prominent among them. But Sullivan was born and bred in Massachusetts, and that was where he wanted to stay.

In 1969 the Patriots played at Sullivan's alma mater, Boston College (he was in the class of 1937), then moved to historic Harvard Stadium in 1970. It was there that one of the more humorous incidents in the team's history occurred.

On the day of the season opener against the Dolphins, controversial coach Clive Rush cut two players because of contract disputes, leaving a couple of roster spots open just hours before the game. A few days earlier Rush had released Bob Gladieux, a running back from Notre Dame, who enjoyed having a good time and a few drinks. Gladieux was nicknamed "Harpo" after one of the Marx brothers because of his frizzy blond hair and crazy antics. And rather than mourning over the apparent demise of his professional football career, Gladieux instead decided to throw an Irish wake, which extended over several days and a variety of watering holes across the city.

When Sunday rolled around, Gladieux—although not entirely steady on his feet—and a buddy decided to go to the opening game to cheer on his former teammates. It was a warm, pleasant day and as Gladieux was once again getting thirsty, his friend volunteered to go to the concession stand for beer. While

Harpo's Story

The story of Bob Gladieux, the man who came out of the stands to make a tackle on the opening kickoff of the 1970 season opener really starts, he says, two years earlier. "The same thing happened to me two years in a row," Gladieux says. "My rookie season, it's on Thursday of the final week of the preseason, when 'The Turk' usually comes round, taps you on the shoulder, and tells you to bring your playbook. That never happened. I practiced that day, showered, and went back to my room happy as a lark. I called my family and friends, and told 'em I'd made the team.

"After that, I turned on the television to see the news, and I was watching the sports when I heard, 'Bob Gladieux was the last Patriot cut.' I wondered what the hell was going on. That crushed me. I was despondent. Heartbroken. Angry.

"I rushed over the next morning to see the coach, Clive Rush. He said, 'Bob, I'm terribly sorry. I wish I could have gotten in touch with you. But we had some decisions we had to make and went another way. But we'd definitely like to have you on our taxi squad, and there's a good chance we'll bring you back next week.'

"Now, while I'm sitting there, the hold light on his phone is blinking. He points to it and says, 'If you don't want to be on our taxi squad, I've got a guy from the Jets who'd love to take your spot.'

"I said, 'Coach, I just want to play. I'll do whatever you want me to do.' I was on taxi squad for just one week, then they brought me back and I played the whole season. I played a little bit at halfback, but my forte was special teams.

"My second year, I had an excellent camp. It came down to the final day again. I practiced that Thursday, and nobody said a word. I had an apartment then, and went home and called my family and friends. Then I picked up a paper that evening and read, 'Bob Gladieux, halfback, was cut.' I said, 'This is a bunch of crap. I'm fed up with this operation.'

"I knew the ropes of the city by then, so I went downtown to have a little libation and do a little dancing. I met a fun young lady, and we had just a rock-and-roll time. We rocked and rolled all that night, and then the next two. We had a blast. We partied, and I more or less got rid of my frustration.

"On Sunday morning, I woke up somewhere on Beacon Hill and, all of a sudden, I got sentimental. I thought, 'I've got to go out to Harvard Stadium and see the game.' A friend came by to pick me up. I had a six-pack of tall, sixteen-ounce Schlitz. He'd brought a bottle of homemade port wine. When we got to the stadium, I bought a program, showed an usher my picture, told him the story of what happened to me, and he let me in for free. So we go in, and I tell my buddy, 'You get the first round, I'll get the second. And don't forget to put mustard on my hot dog!'

"He'd gone to the concession stand when I suddenly hear: 'Bob Gladieux, please report to the Patriots dressing room.' I thought I was dreaming. I look up and, I swear, it was a blue-grey sky, just like in the story Grantland Rice wrote about the Four Horsemen. I look up at that sky, and it's like God telling me to report.

"But then I think, 'Maybe He's punishing me for being mischievous.' That's when the lightbulb went off in my head. And it had a dollar sign on it. I said to myself, 'Do it for the money, you damn fool. They've been shafting you for two years. Now you can get something out of them.'

"So I dart out of the stands and down to the locker room. Clive says, 'You're activated. Get dressed.'

"I've got about five minutes to get my pads and uniform on and get out on the field. I'm still tying my britches when they send me out to cover the kickoff. Normally I'd be saying to myself, 'Okay, go down and bust the hell out of the wedge and make the tackle.' Instead, I'm thinking, 'Whatever you do, Harpo, protect yourself. Avoid all contact. Don't get hurt.'

(continued)

> "We kick off and, as I head down the field, the wedge is coming straight at me. Now, while I'm running, my buddy has come back to our seats with the beers and hot dogs. He's asking people, 'Where's the guy who was sitting here?' They told him I'd left, and he was wondering, 'Where the hell did Harpo go now?'
>
> "Meanwhile, I want nothing to do with the wedge, so I run around it to the left side. The ball carrier went around the right side and ran right into my arms. That's when my buddy hears the PA announcer say: 'Tackle by number 24, Bob Gladieux.' I think he spilled the beer.
>
> "Year after year, the more I think about it, I wonder how the hell I did it."

he was gone, there was an announcement made over the stadium's public-address system: "Will Bob Gladieux please report to the Patriot locker room?"

At first Gladieux wasn't entirely sure he wasn't suffering from delirium tremens. He had no doubt that he was in no condition to play. But hey, if his team needed him, well—he was after all, and above all else, a football player. So off he went to the Patriots' locker room, where Rush told him to get a uniform on—he was back on the team.

Down on the field the Dolphins won the coin toss and elected to receive. The Patriots kicked off, and moments later the PA announcer boomed: "Tackle by Bob Gladieux." Inspired by

Harpo's heroics, the Patriots went on to win, 27–14. It was one of only two victories the team had that season.

Sullivan continued to fight a losing battle for a stadium—an issue that was becoming critical because of the merger that year of the AFL with the NFL, which required teams to play in stadiums with a seating capacity of at least 50,000. In the early months of 1970, a proposal to build a domed stadium along the Neponset River, near the Quincy line, was being debated by the Boston City Council. Ron Hobson, a sportswriter for Quincy's evening newspaper, the *Patriot-Ledger*, who had covered the team since 1961, had lunch that winter with a friend who was a council member. "He said to me, 'Off the record, there'll never be a stadium built within the confines of the city of Boston,'" Hobson said. "'No neighborhood will accept it. It'll never happen.'"

At the time Hobson also was working as publicity director for Bay State Raceway, a harness track owned by E. M. Loew, the movie theater magnate, along Route 1 in Foxboro. There was abundant open land surrounding the track, which was located about halfway between Boston and Providence. Hobson suggested to his father, Press, who was general manager of the track, that perhaps Sullivan would be interested in building a stadium on the site.

"I called Billy," Hobson said, "and two days later, he came down for a visit. He'd always been adamant about building in the city of Boston, and there had been a number of proposals over the year. But he fell in love with the idea. The Neponset deal fell through, as expected, and that's how the ball got rolling."

Loew donated the land to the town of Foxboro in exchange for receiving the parking revenue on game days. "He could see

Owner Billy Sullivan (left) admires a model of Schaefer Stadium with other executives in 1971. AP/Wide World

dollar signs in the parking lots," Hobson said. The town, in turn, leased the land to Sullivan in exchange for, initially, 25 cents per ticket sold. Construction began that summer and, amazingly the stadium was ready to open in time for the 1971 season. Well, almost ready.

Built for less than some teams now pay their quarterbacks— a mere $6.7 million, privately financed through the sale of stock in Stadium Realty Trust—the stadium had no frills, few amenities, and fewer creature comforts. But there was hardly a bad seat among the 61,297 in the house, although most of them were aluminum benches that were, as Gil Santos said, "hot as hell in summer, and freezing cold in winter." Humble though it was, it was—at long last—a permanent home for the Patriots. And there was no place like it. Fortunately.

The grand opening of the stadium, which was called Schaefer Stadium after Sullivan sold the naming rights for $1 million to the brewing company, always will be remembered in New England for creating the mother of all traffic jams. Accessible only by a north-south highway with just two lanes in each direction, it not only was difficult to get to the stadium, but the parking was found to be inadequate for the capacity crowd that showed up for the first preseason game against the New York Giants.

"Looking up and down Route 1," Santos recalled, "I could see a seemingly endless line of car headlights." The line never seemed to move.

"There was no room in the parking lots," Santos said. "It was a disaster. I still run into people who tell me they heard the entire game on the radio while sitting in their cars, within sight of the stadium."

The fans lucky enough to get in weren't so fortunate afterward, when they found they couldn't get out. "I don't remember what time I got home, or how long it took," said Santos, "but I know it was real late."

Traffic wasn't the only problem the Patriots had with backups. "The most bizarre, and funniest, thing in all my years with the Patriots," Santos said, "was 'The Big Flush.'"

It was during that Giants game that the Patriots discovered they had a giant water-pressure problem at their new stadium. There were, to be polite, problems with the plumbing. And not just because some irate plumbers, angry over contract issues, had installed some urinals so high that they were unusable to anyone under 6 feet tall. (Patriots wide receiver Randy Vataha, who was 5'8", used to complain that he had to ask a teammate to pick him up in order to use the facilities in the team's locker room.)

The toilets that were reachable overflowed, and the town of Foxboro also had concerns that, because it never had to deal with sudden water use by as many as 60,000 people in the span of a few hours, there might be difficulties if, say, a fire broke out in town and large quantities of water under high pressure were required to extinguish the flames. "The town's board of health was going to withhold its permit," Santos said. "The next game was in jeopardy."

The Patriots had two weeks to solve the problem. A water tank quickly was installed on the premises and then, the day before the next game, the team scheduled what has come to be known in Patriots lore and legend as "The Big Flush." "It was scheduled for a Saturday," Santos said. "They wanted to see if everything worked properly, with every toilet and urinal being flushed at the same time. That would never happen during a game, but they wanted to test the system under the most extreme circumstances."

In order to run the test, the team recruited sportswriters who covered the team, including Hobson and the late Will McDonough, prominent columnist for the *Boston Globe* and NFL analyst for CBS. Santos, of course, was there too. "They wanted as many people as they could get," Santos said, "in order to be able to flush all the johns. I signed on because it was a story, and because I was the voice of the team. I figured I could kill two birds with one stone. One, I could get a story. And two, I'd find out if everything worked.

"It was set up like a military operation. We were divided into platoons and were stationed all along the concourse level. Each of us was assigned a bathroom. We stood at the entrance of our designated restroom, poised and ready for action.

"There were people with whistles and, when they blew them, we had been instructed to run into every men's room, every ladies' room, turn on the faucets and flush every urinal, every toilet, as fast as we could. When the whistles blew, off we went, flushing like mad and laughing like hell.

"When it was over, they announced the operation had been a success."

A Different League

It truly was a different league. "The NFL didn't want to acknowledge us. They ruled the roost. They wanted us to fail and go away," said Gino Cappelletti, who is one of only three players to have played in every game in the colorful ten-year history of the American Football League. Many of the players who were in the AFL in the league's early years had been sent packing by various NFL teams, and Cappelletti was no exception. Rosters were much smaller then—thirty-three players, as compared with fifty-three now—and so was the annual turnover.

"In the NFL of the late '50s and early '60s," Cappelletti said, "very few rookies would make the roster—maybe three or four a year. I had a tryout with the Lions as a quarterback. But they had Bobby Layne and Earl Morrall, and I didn't have a big arm. I didn't get to stick around long enough to show them what I could do as a kicker."

Cappelletti bounced around for a few years after that, doing a hitch in the Army, and then playing briefly in the Canadian Football League. When, in the summer of 1960, he was offered a shot with the Patriots in the upstart AFL, he quit his job as a bartender in Minneapolis and headed for Boston. And there he became one of the best players, not just in Patriots history, but also in AFL history.

Not that anyone—least of all Cappelletti—had any inkling of that when he reported to training camp at the University of Massachusetts, in Amherst, that first summer. He wasn't thinking about making history at that time. He was just worried about making the team. "All of the guys who came into the AFL had a passion for football," he said. "They had to, because there was no guarantee the league was going to survive. Everyone was trying to find their identity as football players."

Cappelletti certainly was. He had been a quarterback in college at Minnesota in the Gophers Single Wing offense, where the halfback was the featured player. "I'd been all-state as a halfback," Cappelletti said, "but when I got to Minnesota, they already had Paul Giel, who was an All-American." (Giel went on

Gino Cappelletti was a standout on the Patriots during the AFL years.
AP/Wide World

to play professionally, but not in football. He also was an outstanding baseball pitcher, and he signed with the Giants and spent six seasons in the National League.)

"After a little while," said Cappelletti, "[Coach] Wes Fesler said to me, 'Gino, we've got to talk. I want you in the lineup. But if you want to play halfback, it could be a while, because you're behind Giel. I'd like to see how you look at quarterback.'"

So Cappelletti, displaying the versatility—and the willingness to do what was best for the team—that later would make him a star for the Patriots, moved to quarterback, where he blocked for Giel, caught a few passes, and occasionally carried the ball.

When he reported to camp with the Patriots, Cappelletti knew he wasn't good enough to make it as a quarterback, even in the AFL. So he decided to try out as a defensive back. "You were constantly checking the lists," he said of that first training camp at the University of Massachusetts. "I mean, they used to post cut lists between workout sessions. If a coach passed by and said 'Hi,' you felt on top of the world. If he passed without saying anything, you figured you were on the next van out."

Those vans logged a lot of miles.

"They always used to talk," said Tom Yewcic, who played quarterback and punted for the Patriots for six seasons in the early 1960s, "about the three teams at the Patriots' camp—one going to the airport with players just released, another arriving from the airport with a new bunch, and the one on the practice field. You made sure not to get to know anybody real well."

There really wasn't much chance of that. "We must have gone through a couple hundred players that first year," Cappelletti said. "There was so much confusion that one guy stayed in

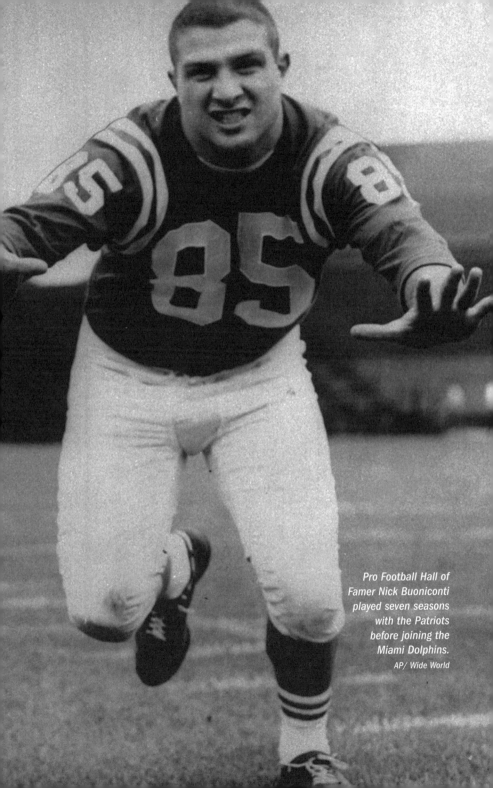

Pro Football Hall of Famer Nick Buoniconti played seven seasons with the Patriots before joining the Miami Dolphins.
AP/ Wide World

camp three or four days after he was cut, until one of the coaches caught him loading up his tray on the lunch line."

Yewcic provided a vivid example of how many players were coming and going in those days. "My first four games, the guys who had lockers on either side of me changed with every game," he said. "That was eight new guys in four games."

In later years, though, when the league achieved more stability, so did the rosters. "We had a togetherness then that just doesn't exist today," Yewcic said. "It wasn't uncommon to see eighteen or twenty guys go to dinner together on the road."

In the beginning Cappelletti's concern was that he would be told to hit the road. But he managed to stick with the Patriots as a defensive back, and he intercepted three passes in a game against Oakland that first year. He also did the kicking and wound up leading the team in scoring—as he would every season through 1969. "Even as a kid, every team I was on, I wanted to be the kicker," he said. "I'd practice by making a hole in the ground with my heel and kicking the ball. Kicking was my pride and joy. I loved doing it."

But with smaller rosters, teams couldn't afford players who were strictly specialists, and Cappelletti knew it was only a matter of time before the Patriots signed faster, and better, defensive backs.

One day, early the next season, the Pats found themselves down to just two receivers because of injuries. "We only had Jim Colclough and Joe Johnson," Cappelletti recalled. "When we ran pass patterns in practice, we'd have to wait for them to come back in order to run the next play.

"One time, they were slow to get back—they were getting tired, running every route—and I was standing behind the huddle. Butch Songin, our quarterback, started calling the play, even though there was a hole in the huddle, and so I jumped in. He called a pass pattern. I knew it, and ran it. Butch, unknowingly, threw the ball to me, and I caught it. Mike Holovak, who was still the receivers coach then, stopped me as I was going back to the huddle and asked me where I had learned to catch the ball. I told him I'd caught some passes in college. That's when he told me, 'You stay out with me after practice. We need help at that position.'"

And Cappelletti gave it to them. He went on to lead the team in receptions in 1961 with 45, including 8 touchdown catches. He also led the league in scoring with 147 points, kicking 17 field goals and 48 extra points.

Cappelletti went on to become one of the team's all-time bests. And not only was he one of the all-time great Patriots—when he retired after the 1970 season, he was the AFL's all-time scoring leader, with 1,130 points—but the personable Cappelletti also is one of the team's all-time great guys.

He's been around the club for thirty-seven of the last forty-five seasons—eleven as a player, three as an assistant coach under Ron Erhardt, from 1979 to 1981, and twenty-three as the color analyst on the team's radio broadcasts. "I'm proud," he said, "to have played in Boston and in the AFL. When we started, we were just hoping the league could succeed.

"That first year or two, you'd tell people you played for the Patriots, and they'd ask, 'Who are they?' In those days the Giants were the favorite team in New England. They had all the household names—Frank Gifford, Andy Robustelli, Y. A. Tittle, Sam Huff. But, slowly but surely, we started getting our own fans."

Vital Statistics

Gino Cappelletti spent his entire career with the Patriots (1960–1970) and is one of only three men who played every weekend of the AFL's ten-year existence. His jersey—number 20—has been retired by the Patriots. Here are Cappelletti's career statistics:

RECEPTIONS

Year	Number	Yards	Average	Touchdowns
1960	1	28	28.0	0
1961	45	768	17.1	8
1962	34	479	14.5	5
1963	34	493	14.1	2
1964	49	865	17.7	7
1965	37	680	18.4	9
1966	43	676	15.7	6
1967	35	397	11.3	3
1968	13	182	14.0	2
1969	1	21	21.0	0
1970	0	0	—	0
TOTALS	292	4,589	15.7	42

The fans turned out to root for Cappelletti and quarterback Vito "Babe" Parilli, who combined to lead the Pats to the AFL Championship Game in 1963. Defensive linemen Jim Lee Hunt and Houston Antwine also were fan favorites, along with, a little later, running back Jim Nance. "Babe was kind of fidgety and

KICKING Year	PATs	Attempts	Field Goals	Attempts	Points*
1960	30	32	8	22	60
1961	48	50	17	32	147
1962	38	40	20	37	128
1963	35	36	22	38	113
1964	36	36	25	39	155
1965	27	27	17	27	132
1966	35	36	16	32	119
1967	29	30	16	31	95
1968	26	26	15	27	83
1969	26	27	14	34	68
1970	12	13	6	15	30
Totals	342	353	176	334	1,130

*Points total includes touchdowns.

nervous," Cappelletti said. "But he was very adept once he took the snap from center. He could throw the ball. He had a nice touch. And he was always a student of the game."

The game against the Chargers for the AFL title in January of 1964 was played in San Diego. San Diego won going away,

51–10. "They were ready for us with a great offensive team," Cappelletti said. "They had guys like Keith Lincoln, Paul Lowe, Lance Alworth, and John Hadl. We were a blitzing team. We'd blitz, blitz, and then blitz again. We'd gotten by that way the whole year. All the Chargers did was throw short tosses when our guys were blitzing, and there was nobody to make the tackle."

As opponents would learn in later seasons, tackling Nance, a bruising 240-pound back out of Syracuse, was a daunting task. "He was a terrific guy," Cappelletti said. "He had a good sense of humor and was a team guy all the way. As a rookie he came in immensely overweight. He was really lumbering around. He looked bad that first year."

So bad, in fact, that Holovak threatened to make Nance an offensive lineman if he didn't lose weight. "Jim got himself into shape that off-season," Cappelletti said. "And he had a fabulous year in '66."

Nance led the AFL in rushing that season, gaining 1,458 yards on 299 carries and scoring 11 touchdowns. He had 1,216 yards in 1967 and, while he never again surpassed the 1,000-yard mark, Nance led the Pats in rushing every year through 1970. "He really could run it up in there," Cappelletti said. "Guys would be bouncing off him."

Right from the outset, AFL games featured more scoring than those in the established NFL. "The NFL in those days played a grind-it-out, chew-'em-up kind of game," Cappelletti said. "They emphasized defense. We had offenses that were more wide open. Guys like Sid Gilman, who was with the Chargers, believed in throwing the ball all over the field. The NFL was very

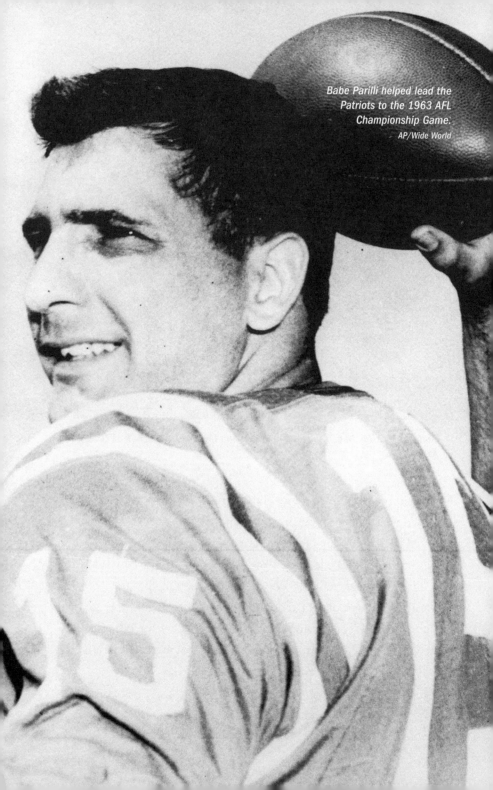
Babe Parilli helped lead the
Patriots to the 1963 AFL
Championship Game.
AP/Wide World

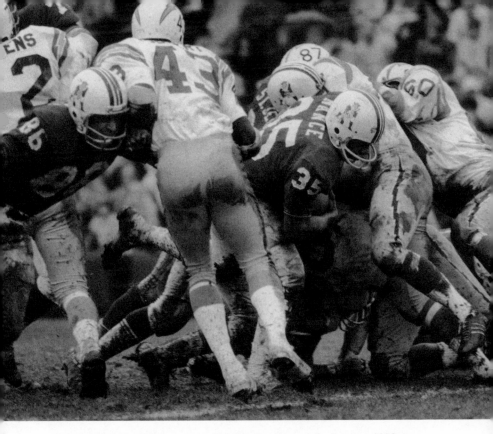

Running back Jim Nance squeezes between San Diego defenders in a 1970 game.
AP/Wide World

critical of us. They'd say we didn't know anything about defense, so we could never measure up to them."

The nation's fans had a chance to make their own evaluation when the AFL landed a network television contract in 1961, the league's second season. "Wisely," said Cappelletti, "they put the games on at four o'clock. People still were hungry for more football after the NFL games, and they said, 'Let's watch the other league.' With all the high-scoring games we had, that appealed to fans."

With each passing year, the popularity of the AFL continued to grow. "Players today wouldn't believe what it was like for us in those days," Cappelletti said. "Everything's plush now. We had one guy to tape everybody's ankles, and there was a time when we watched game film on bedsheets while sitting on milk cartons. We didn't always know where we were going to play, or where we would practice.

"But all that adversity we went through brought us closer together. We loved the game, loved being part of a team. There was tremendous camaraderie, a feeling of relying on one another, of helping one another. The guys who shared that AFL experience formed bonds that will last forever."

Billy Sullivan

You can't tell stories about the Patriots without a chapter on Billy Sullivan. That's because there would be no Patriots stories had it not been for Billy, whose determination and dedication brought pro football back to New England. The sad part, for those fortunate enough to have known him, is that Sullivan no longer is around to tell those stories himself. He passed away in 1998, at the

Billy Sullivan was the beloved original owner of the Patriots. AP/Wide World

age of eighty-two. On the other hand, given a chance to tell a few tales about his beloved Patriots, Billy could have filled a book so thick it would make *War and Peace* seem like a quick read.

Billy loved to talk, and it was a treat to listen to him spin yarns about his days as a publicity man, first at Boston College, his alma mater (class of 1937); then at Notre Dame; and after that, for Major League Baseball's Boston Braves in the days of "Spahn and Sain, and two days of rain"—the formula that won the National League pennant in 1948.

The patriarch of the Patriots was loquacious and lovable, as well as irascible and combative. He was highly competitive— especially on the golf course, where he delighted in winning a match for even the smallest of stakes—and also, at times, vindictive. There was no middle ground with Billy. If you weren't with him, you were against him. He was a man who, having set himself a goal, worked toward achieving it with single-minded dedication and boundless energy. Someone once described him as being "like sandpaper—he wears you down."

In a war of words, the garrulous Sullivan was a superpower. When it came to opposing views, he was not always a good listener. Of course, if he had listened back in 1959 to what was sound, sensible, and well-intentioned advice, he never would have become the owner of a professional football team.

In the fall of that year, Sullivan had $8,000 in his savings account, money that he and his wife, Mary, had put aside as a down payment on a summer house on Cape Cod. Instead he used it as a down payment on the Patriots.

With that, Sullivan joined seven other men in forming the fledging American Football League. They called themselves "The Foolish Club." And Sullivan, the cash-strapped founder of the Patriots, may have been the most foolish of all. "I was the only man who was not independently wealthy—or," the smiling

The Foolish Club

Billy Sullivan was one of the original owners of the upstart American Football League in 1960 who called themselves "The Foolish Club." Here are the original members of The Foolish Club:

K. S. (Bud) Adams	Houston Oilers
Barron Hilton	Los Angeles Chargers
Bob Howsam	Denver Broncos
Lamar Hunt	Dallas Texans
Billy Sullivan	Boston Patriots
Ralph Wilson	Buffalo Bills
Max Winter and William Boyer	Minneapolis*
Harry Wismer	New York Jets

* Minneapolis withdrew from the league one day before being granted an NFL franchise in January of 1960; Oakland eventually became the eighth team in the AFL's first season.

Sullivan would add, with a squint that only heightened the bright sparkle in his eyes, "even dependently wealthy. At the time I had $8,000 to my name. I hustled around to come up with the $25,000 the league required." That was pocket money for the other owners. While Sullivan was president of the Metropolitan Petroleum Company of Boston, which sold and delivered fuel oil, men such as Lamar Hunt and Bud Adams owned oil wells.

"Boston," Hunt once said, "probably had the most unusual beginnings of any franchise in history. In fact I'd call them very improbable, especially from the standpoint of what we do today— all the research that goes into the people, the city, all those kinds of things. But I guess there never would have been an American Football League if we'd had enough sense to do those things."

A pro football team—even one in an upstart league—was a rich man's toy, an amusement for well-heeled tycoons with family fortunes, such as Chargers owner Barron Hilton, scion of the famous hotel owners. But for the Sullivans, football became the family business. When Billy owned the Patriots, the pictures of the club's front office management that were displayed in the media guide made it look like a Sullivan family photo album.

In 1985, the year the Pats won the AFC championship and went to the Super Bowl for the first time, Billy's oldest son, Chuck, was executive vice president. His youngest child, Patrick, was general manager. Included among the team's board of directors were Billy's wife, Mary; his son, William III; daughters Jeanne Sullivan McKeigue and Nancie Sullivan Chamberlain; Billy's sister, Mary; and his cousin Walter.

The nepotism wasn't surprising. His family and his football team were the great loves of Sullivan's life, so it was only natural that the two became inextricably intertwined. Loyalty also was intensely important to Billy, and who could be trusted if not one's family? As Patrick said of his tenure in the team's front office: "I had an advantage over most general managers because I didn't have to justify what I was doing as being in the family's best interests. It was assumed I wouldn't do something I didn't feel was in the family's best interests. To me, winning was in the family's best interests."

Billy Sullivan and his son Chuck (left) hold a sketch of the Patriots' new stadium in 1983. AP/Wide World

Billy Sullivan always had a keen interest in sports. His father, William H. Sr., had been a reporter for the Lowell, Massachusetts, *Sun*. Billy paid his way through Boston College by "stringing" for his hometown paper. He later used those writing skills to ghost-write a nationally syndicated column for Frank Leahy, Notre Dame's football coach.

Sullivan, then a recent graduate working in the office of sports publicity, met the legendary Leahy when Boston College gave him his first head-coaching job in 1938. "I remember so well the headline when [Leahy] left Fordham to begin his incredible success story at Boston College," Sullivan wrote in the foreword to *Shake Down the Thunder*, a biography of Leahy written by Wells Twombly. "The words screamed forth: 'Unknown Leahy Signed by Boston College.' When I met him, he looked at me and said, 'How do you do? I am Unknown Leahy.'"

Leahy wasn't unknown for long, as he led BC to back-to-back bowl games in 1939 and 1940, completing an undefeated season in the latter with a victory in the Sugar Bowl over Tennessee.

Sullivan's long association with Leahy paid dividends when he was trying to land an AFL franchise. "He never forgot someone who stood at his side," Sullivan wrote. "It was 1959, and the American Football League had just been formed. It had granted seven franchises, and the expansion committee consisted of Frank, then general manager of the Los Angeles Chargers; Harry Wismer of the New York Titans; and Lamar Hunt of the Dallas Texans.

"I knew Wismer well because he did the broadcasts of Notre Dame games when I was there working with Frank. But Lamar Hunt didn't know me whatsoever. Many cities were being considered. . . . At the last moment I got on the telephone and told [Leahy] that I had a group put together that had enough money to make the project a success. There was one major objection—we had no place to play. I was quite worried about that situation.

"I should have known [Leahy] better than that. I learned later that, out of loyalty to me, he contacted each of the club presidents and persuaded them that Boston should have a team, even though there was no place to play, and even though the Boston Redskins, Boston Bulldogs, and Boston Yanks had all

Patriots Ownership History

The Patriots have had four owners in their forty-five-year history:

PRINCIPAL OWNER	YEARS
Billy Sullivan	1960–87
Victor Kiam	1988–92
James B. Orthwein	1992–94
Robert Kraft	1994–present

failed in less than two decades. Frank Leahy was a most persuasive man."

So, too, was Sullivan. And tough. And tenacious.

He nearly lost the team in a power struggle with other stockholders in 1974. Instead of taking a profit and leaving the game, Sullivan battled to regain control of what he always considered his club. "I had my whole life tied up in the team," he said. "I felt it was worth fighting for." In order to buy out the disgruntled partners, Sullivan had to raise more than $11 million. "That shows you how smart I am," he said. "I owned the whole thing for $25,000, and it cost me $11 million to get it back."

Although he came out ahead in the long run, the real beneficiaries of Sullivan's tenacity were the fans of New England. Despite his ongoing financial struggles and the constant rebuffs he endured while seeking to build a stadium in Boston, he always spurned offers to move the team. He not only brought pro football back to New England, but he also made sure it stayed there. "My father took a hell of a gamble when he bought the franchise," Pat Sullivan said. "All the sportswriters—and they were all friends of his then—thought he was a fool. But he pulled it off."

He pulled off something else, too. Billy and Mary eventually did buy that house on the Cape—a gorgeous waterfront estate on seven acres in Cotuit.

Remembering the '70s

They may have been the most talented team never to win a playoff game. There was left guard John Hannah, who, along with Jim Parker of the Baltimore Colts, is generally considered to be one of the two best offensive linemen in NFL history. There was tight end Russ Francis, aka "Kid Charisma," who was admiringly labeled "All-World" by television's Howard Cosell, who, as he so often proclaimed, told it like it was. There was cornerback Mike Haynes, who, like Hannah, now is enshrined in the Pro Football Hall of Fame.

The Patriots of the mid- to late 1970s had Sam Cunningham at fullback, Steve Grogan at quarterback—and this was a time when Grogan still was able to run (12 touchdowns rushing, 18 passing in 1976)—Leon Gray at left tackle, Darryl Stingley and Stanley Morgan at wide receiver, Steve Nelson at linebacker, and Chuck Fairbanks as coach and general manager.

Bad Timing

The Patriots were 11–3 and the AFC wild card team in 1976, and then won the AFC East in 1978. But they never won a playoff game. "It seemed as if, every year, something happened to us," Francis said.

In 1976 the Patriots were victimized in the playoffs at Oakland by highly questionable officiating. "We got robbed," quarterback Steve Grogan said, the disappointment and bitterness still evident in his voice nearly thirty years later. "That team could have won the Super Bowl."

In 1977 New England lost two of its first three games while both Hannah and Gray were missing because of bitter and prolonged contract disputes. And in 1978 everything fell apart just before the final game of the regular season in Miami. "It was weird," said Pete Brock, whose 154 games played as an offensive lineman between 1976 and 1987 ranks ninth on the team's all-time list. "We were called to a meeting before anyone left the hotel. I remember Billy Sullivan standing in front of everyone and explaining how he'd just fired the head coach. That's when we found out that Chuck Fairbanks was gone."

Quarterback Steve Grogan took the snaps for the Patriots in the mid- to late 1970s.
Joe Robbins

"It was a shocking announcement," said linebacker Steve Nelson, who's a coach himself now at Curry College, a Division III school in Milton, Massachusetts. "It totally knocked the whole team for a loop," Nelson said, "because Chuck was such a strong, dominant leader. It was demoralizing. We had such faith in him. We depended on him."

It was Fairbanks, brought in by Sullivan from the University of Oklahoma in 1973 after back-to-back 10–1 seasons and a pair of Sugar Bowl victories with the Sooners, who developed the young talent acquired under the astute eye of Francis "Bucko" Kilroy, the Patriots perceptive personnel expert. The Pats had had six straight losing seasons before Fairbanks arrived, winning more than four games in just one of those years, when they were 6–8 in 1971.

The turnaround wasn't immediate. Although Fairbanks managed to get the Patriots to .500 (7–7) in his second year on the job, they slipped to 3–11 in 1975, and lost their season opener in 1976. Then suddenly it all came together, as the Patriots routed Don Shula's Dolphins, 30–14; went to Pittsburgh and stunned the defending NFL champions, 30–27; and followed that with a 48–17 rout of the rugged Raiders in Foxboro.

Those Patriots were a power team, pounding the ball at opponents with a devastating rushing attack that averaged an amazing 210.6 yards a game on the ground and a stunning 5 yards per carry. They went on to finish 11–3, winning the wild card spot in the AFC and putting the franchise in postseason play for the first time since the 1963 AFL Championship Game against San Diego. "That 1976 team was the best I played on," said Hannah, who spent thirteen seasons in New England, from 1973 through 1985, when the Patriots won their first AFC championship.

Coach Chuck Fairbanks talks with Sam Adams (left) and Leon Gray on the sidelines.
AP/Wide World

That 1976 team may well have been the best in the league—the Patriots themselves certainly felt that way—but they failed to hold a 21–10 lead going into the fourth quarter in Oakland, in part because the Raiders were aided by several disputed calls. There was a noncall when Oakland linebacker Phil Villapiano held Francis, preventing him from making a critical first-down reception. There was a highly debatable, roughing-the-passing penalty on Ray "Sugar Bear" Hamilton, who hit Kenny "The Snake" Stabler just as he was throwing the ball on third and 18 at

New England's 27 yard line with 57 seconds left and the Patriots protecting a 21–17 lead.

At any rate the Raiders pulled out the win, 24–21, when Stabler scrambled over from the 1 with 10 seconds remaining.

The frustration continued in 1977, when the Patriots were unable to overcome the slow start caused by the holdouts of Hannah and Gray and finished 9–5, missing the playoffs. But there was no stopping New England the following year, as they locked up the division title with a week still remaining in the season. And what a week that proved to be, as the story broke that Fairbanks was leaving the Patriots to go to the University of Colorado. "When we first heard the news," Brock said, "guys were standing up and saying, 'Well, we're not playing.' "

Sullivan appointed the Patriots two coordinators—Ron Erhardt for the offense, Hank Bullough for the defense—as co-coaches for the Monday night game in Miami. "Chuck was in a corner of the locker room with Mr. Sullivan," Nelson said. "Billy wanted him to quit. Chuck wanted to be fired, because that way he'd have to be paid. Billy wound up suspending him, and he left the locker room."

"We were stunned," Brock said. "We weren't quite sure how to act. We had two pregame speeches that night—one from Ron Erhardt and one from Hank Bullough." Sullivan could have brought in Knute Rockne, Billy Graham, or any other all-time-great motivational speaker that night, and it wouldn't have mattered.

"I'll never forget that 1978 loss in Miami," said cornerback Raymond Clayborn, who still shares the club record for career interceptions, with 36 (Ty Law equaled it during the 2004 season). "That's when Coach Fairbanks decided to leave the team for Colorado. It was our last game of the year, and we were ready for the playoffs. All of a sudden we had the coach of the team sitting over in the corner of the locker room and two assistant coaches coaching the team.

"I remember Hank Bullough and Ron Erhardt were co–head coaches. While Fairbanks was in the corner of the locker room, they both gave their pregame speeches. Guys didn't know whether to laugh or cry. That really hurt us," Clayborn continued. "It took anything we had out of us for the playoffs."

It was that night that the Patriots went from a powerful team with a shot at the Super Bowl to a disheartened team without a leader. "It was a huge distraction," Nelson said. "It was hard to focus on playing."

The Patriots never did regain their focus. They were easily beaten by Miami, 23–3, and then, even though Sullivan agreed to allow Fairbanks to coach the team in the playoffs, and the Pats had a bye week to regroup, they were trounced by the Oilers, 31–14. There wouldn't be another postseason game played in Foxboro for eighteen years.

The team headed in the wrong direction after Fairbanks's departure. It wasn't until one of his former assistants, Raymond Berry, took over as head coach midway through the 1984 season that the Patriots once again became a playoff team.

"The loss in '76 was more frustrating," Nelson said. "In '78 we lost because of internal problems. In '76 we lost because of external things we had no control over. We had a series of judgment calls that went against us."

Under the easygoing Erhardt, a pleasant man with a gift for designing exciting offenses that could put points on the board both running and passing, the Patriots just missed the playoffs in 1979 and 1980, but then fell apart in 1981, when they went 2–14.

Hall of Famers

Guard John Hannah was the first former Patriot to be inducted into the Pro Football Hall of Fame. Hannah, who played from 1973 to 1985, was inducted in his first year of eligibility in 1991. In all, three former Patriots are members of the football shrine in Canton, Ohio. Nick Buoniconti, a linebacker from 1962 to 1968, who also was a member of the Miami Dolphins "No-Name Defense" of the 1970s, was inducted in 1997. And four years later, Mike Haynes, a cornerback from 1976 to 1982 and a member of the NFL's Seventy-fifth Anniversary All-Time Team in 1994, made it in.

Cornerback Mike Haynes with his rookie-of-the-year trophy in 1976.
AP/Wide World

Deciding the team needed more discipline, Sullivan hired Ron Meyer, who had just brought Southern Methodist back to national prominence thanks to his "Pony Express" backfield of Eric Dickerson and Craig James.

What resulted was a near-mutiny.

Hog

It's a soft summer morning at Patriots training camp, but there's about to be some hard-hitting going on. The offensive linemen gather at one end of the practice field to do some work on a tackling dummy hanging from a metal crossbar between two poles. It's a popular drill with the fans, who gather three and four deep behind a wooden hurricane fence only a few yards away to watch eagerly as these large men block the heavy bag.

One after another, the Patriots linemen settle into their stance, fire out, and hit the dummy, sending it swaying backward. Like a long, weighty pendulum, the big bag swings forward, gathering momentum and force. The players hit it again, and then again, and yet again, but with less power each time. And by the fourth or fifth time, they're not so much blocking the bag as they are fighting it off, straining exhaustedly to keep it from knocking them off balance. At which point an assistant coach steps in, grabs the bag, and signals for the next lineman to take his turn.

Last in line is John Hannah. The crowd presses against the fence, straining forward, eager to get a look at the offensive guard *Sports Illustrated* called the best lineman in the history of the National Football League. The fans are intensely interested in Hannah, expectantly watching his every move. Oh, yeah, they

John Hannah poses with his bronze bust after being enshrined in the Pro Football Hall of Fame. *AP/Wide World*

know they're gonna see something special now from the man they lovingly call "Hog."

But Hannah is oblivious to their attentions. As he always is on a football field, he is all business. He is as focused on the bag as the crowd is on him, and as he hunkers down into his stance, his eyes narrow, his jaw is clenched, and his breath comes in short bursts, like the snorts of a powerful bull, preparing himself to charge.

When the whistle blows, Hannah moves his 285 pounds in a stunning blur, and the bag is sent soaring, higher than before, as if struck by a cannonball. As it begins its slow descent, Hannah is crouched low, hands in front of his chest, his legs moving like pistons, and he is exhaling in loud puffs, like a steam locomotive, gathering speed. Wham! Hannah slams into the bag a second time, sending it even higher.

Down, down, down, the bag comes and then—bam!—up, up, up it goes again.

Unlike his teammates, Hannah isn't getting tired. He's just getting into the flow. Sweat is beginning to pour off him. His face is red. His eyes are mere slits, but with a glint emanating from them as sharp as a laser beam. He can't wait for the bag to come back to him so he can hit it again—harder, and harder, and harder still.

And a funny thing is happening to the crowd. Without realizing it, they have begun to back away from the fence. With each ferocious hit by Hannah, the fans unconsciously edge away. Boom! And they shuffle back another half step, partly in awe, partly in instinctive self-protection, the way you'd keep a respectful distance from a waterfall or a roaring fire.

Even the tackling dummy, inanimate though it is, seems to sense danger awaiting. After each devastating blow, it appears to hang longer at the top of its upward path, as if dreading to go down again and absorb more punishment.

Hannah strikes it again, and again, and again, gathering force, the resounding "pop" of contact growing louder each time. It is the only sound that can be heard, as the crowd has grown strangely silent.

When the coach steps in this time, it is the bag that is being given a needed respite, not the player. That's when the crowd surges forward, when it finds its collective voice: "Yeah, John! Way to go! Way to hit!"

Hannah, who retired in 1985 after helping the Patriots win their first AFC championship in his thirteenth season, always was a hit with New England fans. No one who saw him ever will forget his awesome talent and relentless desire. "His physical ability was unbelievable," said Pete Brock, who played center for the Patriots from 1976 through 1987. "He could just blow people off the line of scrimmage.

"He was built to be an offensive guard. With his strength, physique, and passion for the game, he was the best offensive lineman I've ever seen. One of the other intangibles John had," Brock added, "was that he was never complacent about his ability to play football. He always wanted to be better. Because he worked so hard at being better, he made others realize what they needed to do. If a guy that good was working that hard, how could they do any less?"

Hannah could strike fear into opposing defensive players. "He wore the smallest helmet he could squeeze onto his head," Brock said. "His face would be all squished up, his eyes would narrow, and the veins would start popping out in his neck." And Hannah seldom said much during a game.

"But I remember one time we were playing at Seattle," Brock said. "The Seahawks played a 3–4 defensive front, and they had a linebacker named Michael Jackson, who used to hang a towel from his waist that hung almost to the ground. Jackson was a finesse player. He relied on speed rather than power. Because Seattle played a 3–4, John would come flying out of his stance at Jackson. But instead of taking on the block, Jackson would 'olé' him, stepping aside to avoid contact. Jackson wasn't making any tackles, but John wasn't able to get a good lick on him.

"After a quarter-and-a-half, John was frustrated and furious. He turned to me in the huddle and said, 'That SOB won't let me hit him.' To John, that wasn't courageous. That wasn't how you were supposed to play the game."

Brock would know, because nobody ever questioned his toughness, either. In a game against the Dolphins in Foxboro in 1983, he injured his knee on the first play. "I went back to the huddle," Brock said, "and told the guys, 'I screwed up my knee'— although I might have said it differently. John looked at me and asked, 'Have you got another play in you?'

"I said, 'I believe I do.' Except on that play my knee locked up. I managed to limp back to the huddle and John asked me again, 'Have you got another play in you?' Fourteen plays later, we put the ball in the end zone. I played the entire game, and after every play, John would ask, 'Have you got one more in you?'

"At halftime the doctors told me, 'You can't go any more.' I said, 'Why not? I played one half, I can play another.' I wound up making hamburger of the joint. Thank God for Celebrex. Every time I meet someone from Pfizer, I genuflect. Well, as much as I can."

1985–A Championship Year

To many of his players, Ron Meyer came across as a combination of Captain Bligh, George S. Patton, and The Grinch Who Stole Christmas. After New England's 2–14 disaster in 1981, the trip to the sixteen-team playoff tournament in the strike-shortened 1982 season should have been a ride on the *Good Ship Lollipop*. Instead, the Patriots sounded as if they had been shanghaied aboard the HMS *Bounty*.

There was irritation over petty rules—such Meyer mandates as no popsicles during breaks at training camp, no sitting on helmets on the sidelines, no leaving the hotel grounds the night before the game, and the requirement that offensive and defensive players ride on the buses designated for their specific units en route to the stadium for games.

The grumbling began during Meyer's first summer in 1982, especially among the veterans, and only grew louder. "I made the mistake," he said, "of not communicating as well as I should. I felt I explained the 'whys' of what I was doing clearly enough. But I guess I misread that. I assumed the players understood why I was putting restrictions on them.

"I don't think I was repressive. But the players didn't know me. They didn't understand me. Change is tough on everybody. All egos—including Ron Meyer's—are temperamental. I didn't take that into account with some of the established players."

The veterans, used to a more relaxed, laid-back atmosphere, rebelled at the regimentation instituted by Meyer, a man they felt had been successful at the college level because of his recruiting ability, rather than his coaching skills. "I don't go around looking to play Gestapo," Meyer said. "I don't envision myself as a heavy."

But he was perceived that way by many of the players after Sam Cunningham was fined $1,000 for being tardy in returning to the team after going to California for his mother's funeral, and Vagas Ferguson was fined the same amount for walking off the field because he was tired of having Meyer shout obscenities at him.

Stanley Morgan complained that not enough passes were thrown to him, especially deep balls. Warned by Meyer to keep his mouth shut, Morgan was dubbed "First Amendment Stanley" by his teammates because he no longer had freedom of speech. And John Hannah became so fed up, he said he'd rather retire than play for Meyer.

As it turned out, it was Meyer who was sent packing, midway through the 1984 season, even though the Patriots were 5–3 at the time. Meyer was constantly going to general manager Patrick Sullivan and Dick Steinberg, who was in charge of personnel, and insisting they trade players who were giving him trouble. "Ron eroded his own control over the football team," said Sullivan, "by coming in virtually every week and demanding we trade Tony Collins, trade Stanley Morgan, trade John Hannah. He claimed they were dissidents in the locker room. We were in a situation, frankly, where we had lost confidence in his judgment."

The final straw came when, without consulting Sullivan or Steinberg, Meyer fired defensive coordinator Rod Rust following a 44–24 loss at Miami. "You have to discuss the ramifications of something like that before it's done," Sullivan said. "It was at that point we felt the distractions and turmoil of the type that had developed were not in the best interests of the Patriots. We felt we needed a stable situation."

The man brought in to stabilize the tumultuous situation was Raymond Berry, a Hall of Fame offensive end for the Baltimore Colts, where he was the favorite receiver of the legendary Johnny

Coach Raymond Berry led the Patriots to an AFC championship and to Super Bowl XX.
AP/Wide World

Unitas on championship teams that rank among the greatest in NFL history. An assistant coach under Fairbanks and Ron Erhardt, Berry had been out of football for two and a half years when the Patriots asked him to return to New England. He'd never been a head coach. But he was a calming influence and respected by the players for his demeanor, his football knowledge, and because he had been one of the game's great players.

"My job," Berry said, "is to make something good out of a bad situation." He did much more than that.

Berry took the Patriots to their first Super Bowl in his first full season as head coach in 1985. And he did it the hard way—winning three consecutive playoff games on the road. In 1986 he led them to the division title.

"Raymond made us believe," cornerback Raymond Clayborn said. "When we were 2–3 early in that 1985 season, we had doubts. But Raymond didn't have any. He kept telling us we were good enough to beat anyone if we pulled together."

"Coach Berry," said wide receiver Cedric Jones, "emphasized putting the team ahead of yourself, an unselfish type of attitude. We formed a type of brotherhood, a cohesiveness we didn't have before. Guys really cared about each other. When Raymond took over the job, he talked about a family relationship among players as something we would have to have if we were going to be a championship club."

"He's a really good person," linebacker Steve Nelson said of Berry. "He's a very religious man. He's driven by his beliefs. He believed there was a reason he'd been called back to the NFL, that it was the place he was meant to be at that time. He felt it was his responsibility to give us his best effort."

Berry expected the same from his players. "He treated everyone like a man," Nelson said. "He assumed you'd try to do the right thing. He assumed we had the same goals he had—to win every game."

Silent Treatment

Raymond Berry had a unique way of coaching. After practice one day at training camp, he gestured toward Russ Francis, the Patriots "All-World" (as television broadcaster Howard Cosell liked to call him) tight end. Francis stopped on his way off the field, wondering what Berry wanted. Without speaking, Berry threw a football to Francis, who caught it and held it expectantly in front of him.

Berry then signaled with his hands for Francis to throw the ball back. When Francis did, Berry caught it, then tucked it away, cradling it under his armpit. Looking meaningfully at Francis, but still not saying anything, Berry threw the ball back to him. Francis caught it, and again held it in front of him, a bit quizzically this time. Berry held up his hands. Francis threw him the ball. Berry caught it, and tucked it safely under his armpit.

For the third time, Berry threw the ball to Francis, who, this time, tucked it away after catching it, as if ready to run upfield and take on a would-be tackler. Berry nodded, a slight smile on his face, turned his back, and walked away. Francis smiled, too, shaking his head slightly. Without a word, Berry had gotten his message across—Francis had fallen into the bad habit of being negligent about securing the ball after making a catch.

As kind, thoughtful, and considerate as he was, Berry also was a fierce competitor. Not an exceptional athlete, his success as a player was the result of diligent practice and meticulous preparation, which extended to washing and ironing his own uniform pants so they'd fit properly.

He ran his routes so precisely that, according to a story often told in Baltimore, he was surprised one day in practice when he cut to the sideline to catch a pass and found he was a step out of bounds when the ball arrived. Berry asked to run the route again. When the same thing happened, he went to look for the groundskeeper, who had only that day relined the field. "You measured incorrectly," Berry told him. "The field isn't the right width." A tape measure was brought out, and Berry was correct.

"Raymond was an unusual guy," Pats center Peter Brock said. "But he also was a guy with credibility, a guy you could trust. Playing for him, you got the feeling that you didn't want to disappoint him. I always felt like I wanted to prove to him that I could have played with him on those great Colts championship teams of the late '50s."

There was no indication at the beginning of the 1985 season that the Patriots were on the brink of an AFC championship. As it was, they barely slipped into the playoffs, securing a wild card spot only by beating Cincinnati in the final game of the regular season. "We had to struggle to get into the playoffs," Nelson said. "We were the last seed, so we had to go on the road for all three games. The probability of winning three playoff games on the road isn't very good."

But the Patriots were good enough to pull it off. They beat the Jets in New York, 26–14, then rallied from a 17–7 deficit to

The Quarterback

John Hannah did many great things for the Patriots during his thirteen-year, Hall of Fame career. But he did one very bad thing to Tony Eason. When Hannah once said that Eason "should have worn a skirt," he stuck a very good player with a very bad rap. "I remember the first time I heard he'd said that," said Eason, who learned of Hannah's caustic comment from Les Steckel, who was his quarterback coach with the Patriots under Raymond Berry. "Les was really concerned about it," Eason said. "He said, 'Do you realize how damaging that is?' I said no. I didn't really know."

He learned the hard way.

Hannah's inappropriate—and inaccurate—criticism damaged Eason's reputation severely, leaving a false impression about a quarterback who, until he injured his throwing shoulder in 1987, was as effective and efficient as any the Pats had had up to that time. Eason had been part of the great quarterback class of the 1983 draft, taken in the first round out of Illinois after John Elway, Todd Blackledge, and Jim Kelly, and ahead of Ken O'Brien and Dan Marino.

In just his second season, Eason replaced Steve Grogan as the Patriots starter and threw 23 touchdown passes, with only 8 interceptions. The following year, he led the Pats through the playoffs to the Super Bowl, throwing for 5 touchdowns without an interception in the three road games New England had to win to capture the AFC championship.

The Patriots were last in the league in rushing in 1986, the season after Hannah retired, with a ground game that bordered on the pathetic, averaging fewer than 86 yards a game. Yet, even with opponents knowing he was going to be throwing the ball—many times in unfavorable down-and-distance situations—Eason led New England to the AFC East title. He completed nearly 62 percent of his passes—276 (a club record at the time) of 448—throwing 19 scoring passes and only 10 interceptions.

Any knowledgeable football fan knows Eason couldn't have thrown that many times in so many obvious passing situations without absorbing more than his share of hard hits. But too many New England fans, if asked what they think of Eason, would say, "Wimp." "That was the impression fans had of him, and that was unfair," said Pete Brock, the center who for ten years played alongside Hannah, a legend at left guard.

With a name like Charles Carroll Eason IV, it did seem as if he should be quarterbacking a posh prep school team, rather than the Patriots. And it didn't help that he replaced Grogan. Compared with Grogan, quintessential tough guy Clint Eastwood seems like Pee Wee Herman. Grogan had the lanky build and poker face of a Western gunfighter and played his position just that way. He was willing to take a few shots if he thought he could gun you down.

Eason liked to play it safe. He preferred taking a sack to taking the chance of throwing an interception. It was a style he used to take the Patriots to their first Super Bowl in the 1985 season.

"Steve was much more aggressive in his style of play," Eason said. "He was more of a riverboat gambler-type of guy. He really rolled the dice. My style was more surgeonlike. I liked to pick 'em apart. I wanted to control the clock and not have any turnovers. Looking back at the playoffs, our defense played their butts off, our special teams were awesome—they scored in every game up to the Super Bowl—and our offense was running effectively and didn't turn the ball over."

Despite a pleasant, personable, laid-back personality, Eason wasn't a fan favorite in New England. "When we came back in 1995 to celebrate our tenth anniversary of going to the Super Bowl," Brock said, "the fans booed him. That was unforgivable."

For Brock, perhaps, but not for the easy-going Eason. "I had a good time in New England," he said. "I know I left there under a cloud. But the more I think back on it, when people ask what it was like for me there, I think about the people I got to play with and the games I got to play in. It was a gas."

beat the Raiders in the Los Angeles Coliseum, 27–20, by intercepting three passes and recovering three fumbles.

That sent the Patriots to Miami to play the defending AFC-champion Dolphins, coached by Don Shula and quarterbacked by Dan Marino, in the Orange Bowl, where New England had lost eighteen consecutive games. Despite that long losing streak, the Patriots were confident they were going to win this time. "When we took the field," Nelson said, "we knew we were the better team. We'd beaten them in New England [17–13] in early November, and they'd beaten us in Miami [30–27] in a sloppy game on a Monday night in week 15.

"We matched up well with them. We knew they'd have a hard time stopping us from running the ball, and that they'd have a hard time throwing against us. Clayborn could match up with their two great receivers, Mark Duper and Mark Clayton. With the defense we were running, we needed that.

"Clayborn was unbelievable that day. We left him in man coverage against whichever receiver they sent to his side and pushed all the help to Ronnie Lippett on the other side. Raymond shut down everyone he was up against. I don't think anybody caught a ball on that side of the field all day."

The Patriots, on the other hand, hardly threw the ball. And, when they did, it was for touchdowns. Tony Eason threw three scoring passes, but had a total of just 71 yards passing, completing 10 of only 12 attempts, without an interception. It was a yardage-consuming, clock-eating ground attack that won the game for New England. "The coaching staff, in all its wisdom, and after hours and hours of studying film and strategizing, deter-

Chicago Bears Otis Wilson (55) hits Patriots quarterback Tony Eason in Super Bowl XX. AP/Wide World

mined that Dan Marino had a difficult time scoring from the bench area," Brock said with a wry smile.

"They came to the offensive line and said, 'It's on you.' It had rained earlier that day, and the field was soggy. It was an offensive lineman's dream. 'Oh, boy,' we thought, 'we're gonna run the ball in the mud.' And we did. We knocked the hell out of 'em."

That they did, to the tune of 255 yards rushing on 59 attempts. Craig James ran 22 times for 105 yards. Robert Weathers had 87 yards on 16 carries. Tony Collins added 61 yards on 12 attempts.

It was a huge upset when the Patriots, who had lost eighteen in a row in Miami's Orange Bowl, routed the defending AFC-champion Dolphins, 31–14. "We had the sense," Eason said, "that it was our game from the get-go. We knew that if we laid it on the line, it was our game." "Unfortunately," said Eason, "I think the Bears felt the same way about the Super Bowl." The Chicago defense overwhelmed the Patriots in Super Bowl XX, 46–10.

The Pats jumped out to a 3–0 lead, after which the Bears ran roughshod, scoring 44 unanswered points as New England had no answers for Chicago's dominating defense, nor for an offense featuring Hall of Fame running back Walter Payton and the passing of Jim McMahon. "Everything spiraled downward in a hurry," said Eason, who was pulled in favor of Grogan after failing to complete his first six passes and getting sacked three times. "The wheels came off," he said. "We got our butts handed to us on more than just a couple of plays."

The AFC Championship Game victory in Miami was the biggest win in Patriots history until Super Bowl XXXVI. And, even though the Pats were overwhelmed in Super Bowl XX, that lopsided loss couldn't spoil what had been a remarkable — and remains a memorable — run through the playoffs.

The Patsies

For many—too many, unfortunately—of the Patriots' early years, they were a laughable team. During a particularly pathetic stretch of eleven mostly disappointing seasons, from 1965 through 1975, the Pats finished over .500 only once—in 1966, when they were 8–4–2 under Mike Holovak. In seven of those years, they failed to win more than four games. It was enough to move a devoted fan to tears. Not that the Patriots had many devoted fans—or even all that many casual fans—in those days. But as often as not, what tears were shed resulted from laughter.

Typical of the tragedy-as-comedy that personified the Pats in those days was the near-electrocution of new coach Clive Rush in 1970. The truly shocking incident occurred when Rush stepped to the microphone to introduce the club's new general manager, George Sauer Sr., at a press conference in a downtown Boston hotel.

"As soon as Clive touched the microphone, he screeched," recalled veteran sportswriter Ron Hobson of the *Patriot-Ledger* in Quincy, Massachusetts. "What hair he had on the sides of his head went out in little puff balls. He froze. Couldn't move. Then, when Danny Marr Jr., who was the son of one of the team owners, ran over and pulled the plug, Clive slumped to the floor."

There had been a short circuit in the badly wired microphone, but Rush soon recovered. "They dusted him off," said Hobson, "while he kept saying, 'I'm all right, I'm all right.' When he finally stood up again, that's when he uttered his most-famous line: 'I heard the Boston press was tough, but this is ridiculous.' It was the only funny thing he ever said in his life."

That's not quite true. Rush had come up with a pretty good one-liner a few weeks earlier, when bad weather prevented him from flying into Boston for his own introductory press conference, and he instead had to take a train up from New York. "That's the first time I've ever heard of a new coach being ridden *into* town on a rail," Rush quipped.

Billy Sullivan had decided he needed a new coach after the Patriots went a combined 7–20–1 under Holovak in 1967 and 1968.

His first choice was the legendary Vince Lombardi, who was looking to come out of retirement. But Lombardi, who had stepped down as coach in Green Bay after leading the Packers to victory in the first two Super Bowls, signed instead with the Redskins.

Super Bowl III always will be remembered as the one in which quarterback Joe Willie Namath "guaranteed" that his Jets, 16-point underdogs, would upset Don Shula's heavily favored Baltimore Colts. At the time, Sullivan was very impressed with Shula's defensive backfield coach, a promising assistant by the name of Chuck Noll. But he also was considering Rush, who was receivers coach for the Jets and was reputed to have been instrumental in helping New York's head coach, Weeb Ewbank, put together the game plan that enabled Namath to deliver a shocking 16–7 victory.

"There was always so much negative press in our town about the Patriots playing in a 'Mickey Mouse League,'" Sullivan said. "I was concerned that if we hired Noll, the headlines would be along the lines of 'Losing Super Bowl Coach Hired by Patriots.' It was a dumb decision on my part to base it on that, because Noll actually impressed me more than Rush. Then again, if Noll had come in here and been 1–13, the way he was his first year in Pittsburgh, they probably would have run him out of town."

That was a time when Sullivan was changing coaches even more often than he was changing stadiums. The Patriots went through five coaches in the six seasons from 1968 to 1973, moving from Holovak, to Rush, to John Mazur, to Phil Bengston, to Chuck Fairbanks.

It was in 1971 that the vagabond Patriots finally acquired a permanent home in Foxboro. With his team ready to make the

Owner Billy Sullivan displaying the short-lived, ill-fated new name for his team in 1971. AP/Wide World

move 20 miles southward, Sullivan felt it no longer was appropriate to call them the Boston Patriots. Nor did he want to, since his repeated efforts to build a stadium in that city had been thwarted so many times.

So Sullivan decided to rename his team the Bay State Patriots. But that lasted only until newspapers, always eager to save space, began referring to the team in headlines as the "B.S. Patriots." Given the team's ongoing struggles for respectability, both on and off the field, everyone in New England knew that B.S. did not necessarily stand for Billy Sullivan.

Ah, but the Patriots were a lovable lot, in part because they also were laughable.

There was, for instance, the time when, on a preseason road trip to Buffalo for a night game with the Bills, the players—who'd flown in that morning—were told they would be fined if they disturbed the sheets in the hotel where they'd be spending the afternoon. It seems the team was going to be charged a higher rate if the bedding was disturbed. Adding to the delicious irony of the situation was the fact that the hotel was part of a chain owned by Paul Sonnabend, who was one of the original investors in the Patriots. "We were just going to have a pregame meal there," Gino Cappelletti recalled, "then jump on the bus to War Memorial Stadium.

"It was the first week of August and it was very hot. For some reason we arrived early, so we had to hang around a little bit. Guys were sitting around the lobby or out by the swimming pool. It was so hot, you couldn't believe it. It must have been ninety-eight in the shade. And, in those days, we all were wearing coats and ties, because that was the rule when we traveled.

"Holovak went to talk to the hotel manager. He asked if we could go into the rooms, which were air-conditioned, to watch TV until it was time for our pregame meal. The manager said that would be okay, but added, 'Tell the guys not to get under the covers. If anybody gets under the covers, they'll have to pay for the room.' Well, we jumped at that. Nobody wanted to get under any covers in that heat. We just wanted to watch TV in air-conditioned comfort."

What Larry Eisenhauer wanted, however, was to have some fun. As good as he was as a player—and he was good enough to

They Said It

They were the masters of malaprops. Bucko Kilroy and Ron Meyer weren't always understandable, but they were always quotable. They didn't necessarily make sense, but they certainly were fun to listen to. And when they talked to each other, well, it made for unfailingly interesting, if not entirely intelligible, conversation.

They were together with the Patriots from 1982 through the midpoint of the 1984 season—Kilroy as general manager, then vice president of the team, and Meyer as coach. Here's a sampling of a few of their unforgettable statements:

Meyer, stressing the importance of running practice in a timely manner: "Okay, men, let's simonize our watches."

Kilroy, discussing the possibility of drafting running back Napoleon McCallum: "I really like that Bonaparte kid at Navy."

Kilroy, having heard about an impressive new locker room built by one of the Patriots NFL rivals, made a request of a friend: "Would you take a polio shot of it so I can see what it looks like?"

Kilroy, if he thought something was too expensive, would say it was "cost-prohibited."

Meyer, telling a surprised media corps about an unexpected lineup change: "It's not as if it was carved in blood. It's not like Moses coming down from Mount Sinai with the tabloids."

Even Meyer was confused when Kilroy, talking about the formative days of the Fellowship of Christian Athletes, told him: "Hey, we invented Christianity when I was in Philadelphia."

play defensive line for nine years for the Patriots, from 1961 to 1969—Eisenhauer had many more laughs than tackles.

There was the time when, while riding on the team bus, he decided that Jim Colclough's bright-colored sports jacket was unbearably ugly and proceeded to rip it right off the startled receiver's back. While Colclough was still in shock, and the rest of the players were laughing so hard they couldn't move, Eisenhauer handed over a $100 bill for a new coat.

So it should have come as no surprise to any of the Patriots that Eisenhauer would see the hotel situation in Buffalo as a golden opportunity for misadventure. Politely, he would knock on a teammate's door and ask to come in. When they answered—since he was 6'5" and upward of 250 pounds, there weren't many who could keep him out, even if they'd wanted to—Eisenhauer burst into the room and whipped off the bedclothes, laughing uproariously as he headed down the hall to ambush his next victim.

The best incident involving Eisenhauer occurred in San Diego, at the Stardust Motel in Mission Valley and also involved his father, who was known as "Big Dutch." One of the highlights of the Stardust was the Mermaid Bar, where patrons would sit and watch with avid interest through a plate-glass wall behind the bar as an array of shapely Southern California girls in bikinis performed a nightly water ballet in a brightly lit tank.

"One night," said Cappelletti, still unable to repress a smile as he recalled the events of the evening almost forty years ago, "Larry told all the guys to be sure to go into the lounge for the ten o'clock show and sit up at the bar. We had no idea what he was up to, but we all went in and grabbed a stool. All of a sudden we see two figures dive into the water. At first we couldn't see who they were because of all the bubbles. Then we saw Larry and Big Dutch, swimming underwater.

"Larry takes off his trunks while he's down there, swims right up to the glass, and does a little shimmying and shaking, like the mermaids. And he's got Big Dutch with him. That sort of thing," said Cappelletti, "was commonplace in those days. Guys had a good time. It's too businesslike now."

Funny business was commonplace with the Patriots, although not always intentionally.

There was reason to wonder if Rush still was feeling the after-effects of his near-electrocution when, after losing the first two games of the 1969 season by a combined score of 66–7, he decided to assemble what he called his "Black Power" defense.

"Following the '68 Olympics, where Tommie Smith and John Carlos had given their gloved salute on the medal stand, the idea of 'Black Power' was very big at the time," Hobson said. "Clive put together a defense made up entirely of black players. The problem was that he didn't have enough black defensive players, so he had to shift some guys over from offense to defense."

Not surprisingly, that weakened both units, which weren't any too strong to begin with. "Clive was a strange bird," said Hobson, "sad in many ways."

A couple of the Patriots' lesser talents were also two of the team's biggest characters. Signed in 1979 as a free agent out of tiny Tufts University, located in the Boston suburb of Medford, Mark Buben surprisingly managed to hang on for a couple of seasons with the Pats as a defensive lineman.

One summer at training camp, Buben's roommate was Steve McMichael, another defensive lineman, who'd been drafted in the third round out of the University of Texas. Buben often told the story of how, at the end of the day, McMichael would toss his dirty laundry into a corner of their room. Each day the stack would grow, both in height and odor. As the pile increased, so did Buben's curiosity. When, he wondered, was McMichael ever going to do some laundry?

Finally, McMichael threw the last of his clothing on to the pile, at which point he put one hand on top of the stack, and slipped his other hand underneath. At long last, thought Buben, he's going to go to the laundromat.

Not so. McMichael simply flipped the pile upside down and began wearing the clothes that now were on the top.

McMichael's play in New England wasn't much better than his personal hygiene, so the Patriots cut him. But that apparently served as a wake-up call, because McMichael went on to become a tackle for Chicago's fearsome "46 Defense" that demolished the Patriots, 46–10, in Super Bowl XX in New Orleans.

Buben, alas, is best remembered for the day his voice came booming from the back of the team bus, where a group of Patriots were playing an alphabet game that enjoyed a brief popularity one summer. "I. H.?" he cried plaintively. "I gotta come up with an I. H.?"

According to the rules of the game, Buben was required to name a famous person whose initials were I. H., or be a loser. The derisive hoots of his teammates increased as the seconds ticked past. Suddenly, Buben silenced them. "I got one!" he shouted. "I got one!

"Ivan Hoe," Buben said triumphantly. "You know, Don's brother."

Tight end Russ Francis goes up for a pass against the Baltimore Colts in 1977.
AP/Wide World

Mention of Don Ho naturally brings to mind Hawaii, which then leads Patriots fans to think of talented tight end Russ Francis (who grew up in Hawaii). Francis once explained away his poor play in a game against the Dolphins in Miami as resulting from lack of sleep because the swaying palm trees outside his room reminded him of Hawaii and made him homesick.

It was the legendarily loquacious Howard Cosell who began referring to Francis as "All-World." Unimpressed, Francis's reaction to Howard's hype was, "Just shows you how much he knows."

The truth was that Russell was closer to being out of this world, in many ways. A tremendously gifted natural athlete, the 6'5", 245-pound Francis set a national high school record for throwing the javelin. Among his varied interests were skydiving, motorcycle riding, flying, and scuba diving. He also had a brief stint as a professional wrestler.

Bucko Kilroy, who ran the Patriots drafts so successfully in the 1970s, thought so highly of Francis that he drafted him in the first round in 1975, even though Francis hadn't played football his senior year at Oregon. "The coach, Dick Enright, was a good friend of mine," said Francis, "and the players really liked him. We thought we were ready to go somewhere with him, but we lost the last game of my junior year to Oregon State, and he was fired.

"There just wasn't much of a relationship between the athletic department and players. It wouldn't have been any fun to go back and play under those conditions."

That was a daring decision for a young man who had been named to the All Pac-8 team as a junior and who figured to attract plenty of attention from pro scouts as a senior. "It was my form of protest over the firing," Francis said. "Some scouts told me I wouldn't be able to play in the NFL because of that. They told me I probably wouldn't get drafted. I remember thinking, 'If I don't, I'll do something else.'"

You never knew what Francis would do. He was a three-time Pro Bowl selection and, during one visit to Hawaii for that game, he jumped from the sixth-floor balcony of his hotel room into the pool below. "It was [Steelers linebacker] Jack Lambert's idea," Francis said. "We were talking about diving off the cliffs in Hawaii into the ocean. And he said, 'Yeah, just about that height, too. Think you can do it?'

"So I went over to the elevator and pushed number six. I dove, and when I hit the water, I scraped my knees on the bottom. Sometimes I wonder why I do these things."

Francis was capable of doing wondrous things on the field. He led the Patriots in receiving in 1978 with 39 catches, and he had 41 receptions, including 8 for touchdowns, in 1980. He also could be a fearsome blocker. After leaving New England, he played for the 49ers when they won the Super Bowl in the 1984 season.

Francis felt the Patriots should have gone to the Super Bowl in 1976, when they lost in the divisional playoffs to the Raiders in Oakland. Disturbed because he felt linebacker Phil Villapiano kept holding him, yet never was penalized, Francis nurtured his grudge until years later.

One off-season, when Villapiano was visiting in Hawaii, Francis offered to take him on a sightseeing tour of the islands in his private plane. Villapiano eagerly accepted, only to have Francis flip the plane upside down soon after takeoff. He begged Francis to right the aircraft, but Russell refused, insisting that Villapiano first admit that he had held him in the playoffs in 1976. When Villapiano—who would have agreed to just about anything at that point—readily acknowledged his transgressions and expressed his heartfelt regret, Francis said that wasn't enough and decreed they would remain upside down a while longer as punishment.

Owner and Number-One Fan

Long before he became the owner of the New England Patriots, Robert Kraft was a fan of the New England Patriots. Section 217, row 25, down near the 10 yard line. That's where the Family Kraft sat in the spartan surroundings of Sullivan Stadium, a bare-bones edifice erected in 1971 for less than what Kraft currently pays some of his Patriots players.

Now, of course, Kraft and his wife, Myra, along with their four sons, Jonathan, Dan, Josh, and David, watch their favorite football team play from the luxurious owner's box at Gillette Stadium, the 68,756-seat showplace he built with $225 million of his own money.

"I've always been a fan," said Kraft, who grew up in Brookline, a fashionable suburb of Boston, and followed the fledgling Patriots as they moved from stadium to stadium around the city before finally settling in Foxboro. "Those were wonderful times—driving to the games, tailgating beforehand," Kraft recalls fondly. "It was a great family experience. We became friends with the people in our section. Sports is a great equalizer. It brings people of all backgrounds together—factory workers, business people, black, white—they're all rooting for the home team."

If not for Kraft, there would be no home team in New England. The Patriots would have been long gone, most likely to St. Louis, although there was no shortage of suitors from other cities when ownership of the Pats was very much in play from the mid-1980s until Kraft finally bought the team in 1994.

He always had been more than just a casual fan. "I was passionate," he said, "about the game of football." And like most Patriots fans, he was frustrated by the team's frequent failures. Especially by the fact that, from the time of the NFL merger in 1970 up to the time he purchased the franchise, the Pats had hosted just one home playoff game—and were routed in that one, 31–14, by Houston in 1978.

"As a fan," said Kraft, "I wanted to see my team competing at the highest level." As an owner, that was a goal he was determined to achieve. "I'd always dreamed about buying the team,"

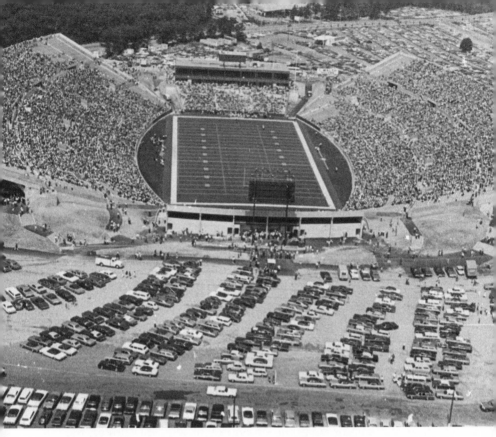

An aerial view of Foxboro Stadium in 1971, the year it opened. AP/Wide World

he said. That was more than merely wishful thinking for Kraft, who not only possessed the financial resources to purchase the Patriots, but also had the business acumen to emerge the winner in a long and convoluted quest to obtain the franchise.

Talk about the "art of the deal." Kraft is a modern-day Michelangelo, but with a briefcase instead of a brush, and the Patriots are his Sistine Chapel—a labor of love that took him nearly ten years to complete, but turned out to be a widely admired artistic success.

Kraft's first step toward buying the team came in 1985, when he purchased a ten-year option on the land surrounding the stadium in Foxboro for $1 million a year. "My banker thought I was nuts," Kraft recalled. It wasn't the last time he would be told that his football flirtations were financially frivolous.

"As in any business," said Kraft, "you're always trying to figure how to get a competitive edge. That option was the first step that allowed me to have an edge. We wound up controlling the parking for all the events at the stadium. We overpaid to get that option in order to have the right one day to buy the team."

Victor Kiam, who proclaimed in television commercials that he liked Remington razors so much that he bought the company, liked the Patriots enough to have bought them from Billy Sullivan in 1988 for $84 million. Sullivan would have loved to keep the franchise in the family, but knew his heirs would be unable to pay the hefty inheritance taxes.

Finances had been a problem for Sullivan from the inception of the franchise, and the situation took a drastic turn for the worse when his oldest son, Chuck, lost millions promoting the eccentric but wildly popular, Michael Jackson's "Victory Tour" in 1984. Deeply in debt Chuck had to put the stadium into bankruptcy, and then up for sale. Because Kiam believed no one would want the stadium without the team—especially a stadium widely recognized as the worst in the NFL—he wound up being shrewdly outbid for the property by Kraft.

"My banker again thought I was nuts, that I was buying a white elephant, that the team would never play there," Kraft said. "But the bankruptcy judge reaffirmed our lease on the stadium through 2001, which turned out to be the year we won our first Super Bowl."

Homes, Sweet Homes

The Patriots moved into 68,756-seat Gillette Stadium in time for the 2002 season, ending a thirty-one-year run at Foxboro Stadium. Here's the club's regular-season record at each of the sites it has called home since the inaugural season in 1960:

Venue	Years	Record
Boston University Field	1960–62	12–7–1
Harvard Stadium	1962, 1970	2–6–0
Boston College Alumni Stadium	1963, 1969	3–5–0
Fenway Park	1963–68	17–16–5
Foxboro Stadium	1971–2001	133–104–0
Gillette Stadium	2002–4	21–3–0

Note. Scheduling conflicts forced the Patriots to play "home" games at San Diego Stadium in 1967 (0–0–1) and at Legion Field in Birmingham, Alabama, in 1968 (0–1); Foxboro Stadium also was known as Schaefer Stadium (1971–82) and Sullivan Stadium (1983–89).

The lease in Kraft's pocket was also his ace in the hole in his high-stakes gamble to buy the team. According to the terms of the lease, if the Patriots were going to play football, it would have to be in Foxboro. Breaking the lease would result in the owner of the team paying treble damages to the owner of the stadium. And by acquiring the stadium, Kraft, who already was garnering the money from the parking lots, added the revenue from concessions, luxury boxes, and stadium advertising, along with more than $1

Owner Robert Kraft has been a Patriots fan all his life. AP/Wide World

million annually in rental fees from the team. "The reason I bought the stadium," Kraft said, "was to try to get into position to own the team."

In 1992 the Patriots were sold again, this time to James Busch (as in beer) Orthwein. He wasn't in the game for the long haul. He was in it so the Patriots could be hauled to his native St. Louis, which had been without a team since the Bidwell family uprooted the Cardinals to Arizona. That the Pats would replace the Cards in the Gateway City seemed a near-certainty after St. Louis failed to get an expansion team, losing out first to Charlotte and then to Jacksonville.

"I was offered $75 million then," Kraft said, "to break the lease. My wife, Myra, said, 'You're going to take it, aren't you?'" Kraft was tempted. He truly was. Until he remembered how he felt as a boy when his beloved baseball Braves abandoned Boston for greener (as in the color of money) pastures in Milwaukee. "A part of me died," he said, "when the Braves left. I regret that to this day. They were my team."

So, instead of pocketing a substantial profit, he wound up paying what then was the highest price ever for an NFL team— $172 million. "This team was gone," he said, "if somebody didn't step up with a good local bid. If we didn't have that stadium lease, there was a high probability this team would have been in St. Louis.

"At Harvard Business School," said Kraft, who earned his master's degree there after graduating from Columbia, "they teach you to buy low and sell high. We broke that rule. But, in this case, it was necessary. This was a unique opportunity, one that required me to stretch beyond what I thought I'd have to. There also were more than twenty pieces of litigation involving the team that we had to take on without having done due diligence. I was the fourth owner in six years. But I realized it would likely be the only chance in my lifetime to do something like this."

It wouldn't be the last time that Kraft, who'd made a fortune as a coolly calculating businessman, would allow his heart to overrule his head when the Patriots were involved. And the fans of New England showed Kraft that his heart was in the right place by lining up in the snow the day after the sale to purchase 5,958 season tickets—a single-day record for the club. The Patriots sold

A New Look

Pat Patriot was much more than merely a team logo. He was a beloved New England icon. If the fans had their way, the crusty, old cartoon character might still be adorning the helmets of the region's favorite football team. He had, after all, been the people's choice when a vote was taken at a game with the Chargers back in 1979.

With design help from the folks at NFL Properties, the Patriots marketing staff had developed a modernistic version of a Minuteman that looked like a colonial-era superhero they dubbed "Super Patriot." Loyalty, however, was important to team owner Billy Sullivan. Pat Patriot had served the club well through good seasons and bad, and Billy wasn't about to toss the old fellow out on his tricorn hat. So he decided to leave the decision up to the fans.

At halftime of the San Diego game, both Pat Patriot and the so-called Super Patriot were paraded in front of the fans. Pat looked like those guys with the fife, drum, and flag from the "Spirit of '76," proud but battle worn. Super Patriot looked like General George Patton on a reviewing stand, all spit and polish.

Much to the surprise and dismay of the marketeers—money had been spent on designing the new mascot—Pat Patriot won in a landslide of such proportions that even legendary Boston mayor James Michael Curley would have been proud. Pat's place in the hearts of the fans, and on the helmets of the Patriots, remained secure after that until James Busch Orthwein bought the team and promptly put Pat out to pasture before the 1993 season.

In was in late March of that year that Orthwein dragged his new coach, a fellow by the name of Bill Parcells, to the posh Four Seasons Hotel overlooking Boston's lovely (although not at that time of year) Public Gardens for a football fashion show. Not only was Orthwein going to reveal the team's new, modern mascot, but he also wanted to show off its new uniforms. Traditionally, and appropriately, a patriotic red, white, and blue, the Patriots would be incorporating silver into their new color scheme.

Silver sells. That was the explanation given by John Bello, a marketing maven at NFL Properties. "What we have done," Bello said, "is contemporize the uniform. From a color standpoint, introducing silver gives a contemporary look. Silver is a hot color."

At the time, Patriots paraphernalia was not a hot commodity. New England ranked twenty-sixth in sales among the twenty-eight NFL clubs at the time, ahead of only Tampa Bay and Kansas City.

(continued)

The Patriots mascot as he looks today. Joe Robbins

"What that tells us," said Bello, "is that something was wrong with what we had."

The real problem was not the Patriots' color schemes, but their offensive and defensive schemes. They had been 2–14 in 1992, after having gone 1–15 in 1990. Which is why Parcells, whose area of expertise was football, not fashion, grumbled, "I don't care about uniforms that make players look good. I want players that make uniforms look good."

As for the new, high-tech Patriot logo, New England fans couldn't decide whether he looked like Elvis in colonial garb or the FTD delivery guy.

"We know," Orthwein said, "that there will be those who will protest this change, who feel it is too drastic a departure from the original. One does not lightly approach changing a team icon. We know we are dealing with a proud history, filled with proud players, with memories that are important to us all. But memories are like looking in the rearview mirror as you drive forward. You can't focus on what's behind. You have to anticipate what lies ahead. We look at this change as evolutionary, not revolutionary. We're not making these changes as a substitute for improving our team. We're doing it in conjunction with improving our team. What you see here is an improvement in the packaging of that product."

To be fair, the new mascot has adorned the helmets of four Super Bowl teams and three NFL championship teams, while the only time Pat Patriot got to the Super Bowl was when the Patriots were mauled by the Bears 46–10. Despite that, if another vote ever were to be taken, it wouldn't be surprising if the fans chose to bring back that quirky old colonial center, crouching over the ball with that cocky smirk on his face.

out every game that season and have continued to do so every year since.

Kraft purchased a team on the rise. To Orthwein's credit he had hired Bill Parcells as coach in 1993. Parcells then used the first overall pick in that year's draft to select strong-armed quarterback Drew Bledsoe.

The Pats, who had gone 2–14 in 1992, the year before Parcells took over, and 1–15 in 1990, made the playoffs in 1994 and then, in 1996, won the AFC championship, beating first Pittsburgh, and then Jacksonville, in Foxboro.

It was a thrill for Kraft to stand on the field where he had watched so many games as a fan and hold the trophy for the conference title over his head in triumph. But the magic didn't last long, as it was revealed during the week before the Patriots were to play the Packers in the Super Bowl that Parcells was going to leave New England to return to New York to coach the Jets.

It shouldn't have been such a shock, because Parcells and Kraft hadn't been getting along all that well. It bothered Parcells that he didn't have complete control over personnel moves. "If they're going to ask you to cook the dinner," he said, "they ought to let you shop for the groceries."

Kraft—correctly, as it turned out—felt Parcells lacked a deep commitment to the franchise. "I was fortunate," Kraft said, "to come in and have one of the great coaches in the game. But, at the core, he really wasn't my kind of guy. I want people who think long-term. Bill is a great coach, but he wasn't willing to make a long-term commitment to the organization. With the salary cap, I've got to make personnel decisions thinking two and three years ahead. He was only interested in coaching year-to-year. Here I was with all this debt, and at the end of every year, he'd drive to Florida saying he'd let me know when he got there if he'd be coming back."

The communication between the two wasn't good. "I wanted to know what was going on," Kraft said. "He wasn't always respectful about telling me what was going on. I'm not taking anything away from his being a great coach. But, if he left to go somewhere else to further his reputation, I'm left picking up the pieces. If you need a quick infusion of credibility, he's great. He brought a lot to this franchise. But he's not someone to manage resources for the long-term."

Kraft accepts his share of the blame for what was an ugly, recriminative breakup. "I made some mistakes, too," he said. "I was a new owner. I was just learning."

Considering that Pete Carroll later won back-to-back national championships as coach at Southern California in 2003 and 2004, it's hard to say his hiring to replace Parcells in 1997 was a mistake. But, hampered by very poor drafts and some key injuries, the team's record slipped all three seasons Carroll was in charge, and after a disappointing 8–8 mark in 1999, Kraft hired Bill Belichick, who hadn't been particularly successful as head coach of the Browns from 1991 to 1995, and who certainly wasn't popular in Cleveland.

"It's my job," Kraft said, "to see things that other people don't. I have certain qualities I look for when I'm hiring someone for an important job. Part of it is a chemistry I personally feel. When Bill was here in '96 with Parcells, we developed what I call 'simpatico.' He impressed me a great deal. Maybe I should have hired him right then. But Parcells had driven us so crazy during the

A view from the end zone in newly constructed Gillette Stadium. Joe Robbins

Super Bowl that I felt anyone who could work with him wasn't right for my system. I wanted a clean break."

Three years later, Kraft broke down and brought Belichick back to New England. "It was amazing to me," Kraft said, "that no one else had hired him. But I was roundly criticized when I did.

"When I hire people, I look first at integrity, character, and loyalty. That's most important. Number two is work ethic. Number three, I look at brains. If they don't have one and two, brains don't matter. Bill had all those qualities, and we've been able to forge a strong, trusting relationship. I'd watched him and the way he worked, and I sensed I'd be able to support him and help him in ways that would allow him to flourish."

After foundering for decades, the Patriots have flourished under Kraft's astute ownership. "I didn't grow up in this business," he said. "I had to learn it. All the businesses I'm in, I try to figure out what I don't know. Once I know what I don't know, I go get the best people who know the things I don't. I wanted an organization that could get to the playoffs every year. Once you do that, anything can happen."

From the standpoint of Patriots fans, the unthinkable almost happened in 1999 when, frustrated by his inability to gain public support for a stadium in Boston, Kraft was on the brink of moving the team to Hartford, which was offering the sweetheart deal of all sweetheart deals. "It was an amazing deal," Kraft said.

Not only was the state of Connecticut going to pay to build the stadium but, Kraft said, the deal also included an agreement that for thirty years the team's revenues would be guaranteed to rank among the top three teams in the league, with any shortfall from the sale of tickets and luxury suites being made up by the state.

It seemed to be an offer Kraft couldn't refuse. But he did. "We had a family meeting," Kraft said. "Five members voted that we stay in Foxboro. One said Connecticut." That one, who, like his father, also has an MBA from Harvard, politely pointed out to his dad, "You just broke every rule of finance."

He was right, of course. But Kraft knew that emotionally, if not financially, he was doing the right thing. "The swing to our family, on a present value basis, was $1.2 billion over thirty years," Kraft said. "Instead of accepting a deal that would have cost us nothing, we went into debt for over $300 million to build our own stadium.

"It was a dumb financial move. But it just felt like the right thing. You know, some things in life aren't about cash-flow statements. The decision wasn't based on money. It was based on quality of life. I knew I'd feel better waking up every day having a stadium close to home. I knew we'd find a way to make it work."

It has worked out exceptionally well, as the Patriots, playing in front of the usual sellout crowds, went undefeated at home in 2003 and 2004.

"The NFL is a tough business," Kraft said. "It's cruel and ruthless in many ways. Harvard Business School doesn't prepare you for it. In our sport, as opposed to some other professional leagues, every team has a chance to win. Oh, there may be three or four teams run in such a way that ownership doesn't really give them a chance to compete. But even poorly managed teams get high draft picks. Eventually, if they get some talent and the right coach, they can do well. Our success hasn't been something that just happened. It's the result of a couple of decades of planning and organizing.

"When I bought the team, I asked the fans to ride along with me. We built this stadium with the fans in mind. I remember sitting on that aluminum bench in the old stadium, freezing my buns off. This stadium and our championship teams are my family's legacy to this region."

Let It Snow, Let It Snow, Let It Snow

Adam Vinatieri always will be remembered for kicking not just one Super Bowl–winning field goal, but two—a 48-yarder as time expired to upset heavily favored St. Louis, 20–17, in Super Bowl XXXVI in New Orleans, and a 41-yarder with 4 seconds left to beat Carolina, 32–29, in Super Bowl XXXVIII in Houston.

But the field goal he'll never forget is the one he made in a swirling snow against Oakland late in the fourth quarter of an AFC Divisional Playoff Game in January 2002. "I'll always remember the Super Bowl kicks," Vinatieri said. "Those are great memories. But if you ask me what was my best kick ever, I'd have to say the one against Oakland, because of the situation and the circumstances."

The situation was desperate, the circumstances dire. "We were down 3 points," he said. "I had to hit it to tie the game. It was snowing. And the field conditions—I don't know if I've ever kicked in conditions worse than that."

Kickoff that cold and blustery afternoon in Foxboro was at four o'clock, and snow had started to fall hours earlier. The game was going to be the last one ever played in Foxboro Stadium, which was to be demolished to make room for the much larger, much better, Gillette Stadium the following season. Work already had begun on the new facility, and so the old concrete bowl sat in the midst of a construction site, surrounded by rutted and rocky parking lots.

Two months earlier, with the Patriots muddling along at 5–5 in late November, the possibility of a having a home playoff game had seemed remote. Especially with young Tom Brady, a sixth-round draft choice in 2000 who'd thrown just 3 passes as a rookie, playing quarterback in place of the veteran Drew Bledsoe, who'd been injured in the second game of the season.

Bledsoe was pronounced ready to play when the Saints came to Foxboro on November 25, but coach Bill Belichick, with his team at .500, decided to stick with Brady. It was a daring decision. And, as it turned out, a brilliant one. The Patriots, behind Brady and a defense that did not allow more than 17 points in any game the remainder of the season, rattled off six straight wins to finish 11–5 and in first place in the AFC East.

Adam Vinatieri's famous kick in the snow against the Oakland Raiders on January 19, 2002. AP/Wide World

So it was that the demolition of the old stadium was put on hold until after the playoffs.

By early afternoon on the day of the AFC semifinal game against the Raiders, the parking lots already were a mass of frozen mud. With a heavy snow beginning to fall, I knew—in fact, I was positive—I was going to be snowed in that night, my car hopelessly stuck in a cold drift, unable to move.

The night the stadium had opened, in August 1971 with a preseason game against the Giants, the Mother of All Traffic Jams had occurred, with cars backed up for miles to the north and south along the woefully, and helplessly, overloaded Route 1. Many fans never made it into the parking lots that night, much less into their seats.

So it seemed almost predestined that, on what would be the final game played at the old stadium, nobody would be able to get out. We'd be trapped, like figures in one of those little snow globes that you shake up and then watch the flakes swirl. It would be so perfectly Patriot-like. Fans couldn't get to the stadium for the first game played in Foxboro. Now they wouldn't be able to leave after the last.

In expectation of exactly that bizarre occurrence, I packed a sleeping bag and a pillow, along with some snacks and a snow shovel, in the trunk of my car. In a worst-case scenario—and Foxboro Stadium was notorious for worst-case scenarios—I could bring the sleeping bag into the press box, spend the night there, then wait for the plows to come in the morning.

It was in such wintry conditions that the Patriots and Raiders—ancient rivals from the days of the AFL—squared off. Through three quarters it appeared as if it would be the Raiders who'd be advancing to the following week's AFC Championship Game. They led at halftime 7–0, and by 13–3 going into the fourth quarter.

But Brady and the Pats kept battling both the Raiders and the elements. While setting club playoff records for passing attempts (52), completions (32), and yards (312), the slow and not very shifty Brady also ran 6 yards for New England's only touchdown, cutting Oakland's lead to 13–10.

New England's hopes for a comeback all but disappeared, however, when Brady appeared to have fumbled the ball away near midfield when he was hit while trying to pass with just 1:43 left in the game. "It depended on the referee's decision whether our season was done," said Vinatieri, who continued to kick balls into his practice net on the sideline while the referee studied the replay endlessly, the snow fell steadily, and everyone else in the stadium waited breathlessly.

When "upon further review," the decision on the field was reversed, and what had at first been ruled a fumble was declared an incomplete pass, Vinatieri, sounding like John Madden, said, "It was a matter of just a few more plays and—boom! Bam!—I was out there."

Out there in the swirling snow, on slippery footing, kicking a hard, cold ball at uprights 45 yards away, with just 27 seconds on the clock and the entire season on the line. Because if Vinatieri missed, the Patriots were done, finished, their playoff hopes gone.

That wasn't the case in either of his last-second Super Bowl kicks, where a miss, while disheartening, merely would have meant the game would go into overtime. Against the Raiders, a miss would send the Patriots home for the season.

"There were 3 or 4 inches of snow on the ground," Vinatieri said. "We were out of time-outs, so we didn't have a chance to clear away the snow from the spot where we wanted to kick." Nor were those the only complications.

Heavenly!

Controversy swirled like wind-whipped snowflakes around another unforgettable game played in the midst of a winter storm in Foxboro. The game would have been memorable in any event, not only because it was an AFC divisional playoff against the Raiders, but also because it was the last game ever played in the old stadium. It was January 19, 2002, and construction already had begun on Gillette Stadium, which would open that summer.

Only two months earlier, the prospect of a playoff game being played in Foxboro seemed highly unlikely. The Patriots were muddling along at 5–5—which wasn't bad, considering that star quarterback Drew Bledsoe had been sidelined in the second game of the season. His backup was a skinny kid who hadn't been drafted until the sixth round in 2000—Tom Brady, out of the University of Michigan. As a rookie, Brady had played in just one game and thrown only three passes. But coach Bill Belichick saw potential for greatness in his young quarterback and kept him in the lineup even when Bledsoe was ready to return in late November.

It was a bold and, as it turned out, brilliant decision, because, with Brady calling signals, the Patriots swept the final six games of the regular season and finished first in the AFC East. That earned them a first-round bye and home-field advantage for the conference semifinal playoff game. Just how much of an advantage that proved to be was debatable, because a snowstorm hit Foxboro that afternoon.

Despite Brady's best efforts—he would set Patriots playoff records by throwing 52 times, completing 32, for 312 yards—the Raiders led, 13–3, after three quarters. But Brady cut the deficit to 13–10 when, after completing 9 of 9 passes in the drive, he scrambled 6 yards for the Patriots' only touchdown. But the game—and the season—seemed to slip away when he appeared to fumble the ball as he was sacked by blitzing cornerback Charles Woodson.

Greg Biker recovered for the Raiders, and with 1:43 left to play and the Patriots out of time-outs, the game seemed to be over. And it would have been, had it not been for rule 3, section 21, article 2, aka "The Tuck Rule," which states: "When a Team A player is holding the ball to pass it forward, any intentional forward movement of his arm starts a forward pass, even if the player loses possession of the ball as he is attempting to tuck it back towards his body."

While the Raiders were celebrating, Coach Belichick was thinking "not so fast." "As soon as I saw the replay," Belichick said, "I said, 'There's no way they're not calling that an incomplete pass' and sent the offense back out on the field. It's absolutely the way the rule is written. It was absolutely the correct call."

Referee Walt Coleman later explained why the original ruling on the field of a fumble was overturned. "From what I saw on the field," Coleman said, "I thought the ball came out before his arm was going forward, so that's why I ruled a fumble. Then, when I got over to the replay monitor and looked at it, it was obvious that his arm was coming forward. He was trying to tuck the ball, and they just knocked it out of his hand. His hand was coming forward, which makes it an incomplete pass."

"Anybody can complain about the rule all they want," Belichick said, "but that's what it is. When you look at the play, that was the correct ruling."

Able to maintain possession, the Patriots wound up tying the game on a tremendously difficult, incredibly clutch, 45-yard field goal by Adam Vinatieri, who then kicked the game-winner in overtime from 23 yards after Brady had put the Pats in field-goal range by completing all eight of his passing attempts in the extra period.

When it was over, Lonnie Paxton, the Patriots deep-snapper, threw himself on his back in the end zone and, like a delighted child, began moving his arms and legs to create "snow angels." It was the perfect image for a team that finds snow heavenly.

"The worse the weather gets," Bruschi said, "the better the Patriots play. When it comes November, December, and the sun goes down, and the snow starts falling, we are extremely confident. That's Patriots weather."

"The job Kenny [Walter, the holder, as well as the team's punter] did was amazing," Vinatieri said. "He had to catch a ball with snow on one end and try to place it as quickly as he could. I was wearing the longest cleats I could get my hands on. They were like shark's teeth. When we went out there, I said to myself, 'Adam, just kick it as best you can.' I tried to stay over my feet, so I wouldn't slip. That's probably why the trajectory was so low."

Aesthetically speaking, it wasn't Vinatieri's best kick. When he hit it, it didn't look high enough or long enough. But it just kept going, and when it wobbled over the crossbar, Patriots fans reacted as if they'd never seen a more beautiful boot. "If you asked me how many times out of a hundred I could make that kick again," Vinatieri said, "I'd be ecstatic if I could make fifty."

Having made that one, there wasn't a snowball's chance in Hades that Vinatieri was going to miss the 23-yarder he hit in overtime to win the game. "A Super Bowl–winning kick is something you dream about all your life," he said. "But I'll never forget that kick in the snow when we beat the Raiders."

Vinatieri's kick was one of just a number of memorable moments the Patriots have enjoyed in the snow. In fact, when the weather has been the most frightful, that's when the Patriots have been particularly delightful. Some of the best games in club history—or, at least, some of the most memorable—have been played in the worst conditions.

Let other cities have their climate-controlled, domed stadiums, where the temperature is always moderate and the wind nonexistent. The hardy—or, perhaps, foolhardy—fans in New England revel in inclement weather.

If you doubt that, consider the scene that took place December 7, 2003, when a blizzard the day before the game against Miami dumped 2 feet of snow in Foxboro, making it difficult for fans to get to the stadium. Those fortunate enough to get into what limited parking spaces were available found that their seats in Gillette Stadium still were covered in snow because there simply was no place to put it. What was shoveled out of one row of seats wound up on top of another.

But when linebacker Tedy Bruschi clinched a 12–0 win with a fourth-quarter interception return for a touchdown, jubilant fans, in a dazzling display of wintry pyrotechnics, spontaneously tossed handfuls of snow in unrehearsed, although seemingly choreographed, unison to the beat of Gary Glitter's "Rock and Roll, Part Two"—bah-dum, bah-dah-dum, hey! (toss snow); bah-dum, bah-dah-dum, hey! (toss snow).

It was beautiful. It was fun. It was quintessentially New England. "Seeing that snow flying got me in the holiday spirit," Bruschi said. "It made me want to go home and sit in front of the fire by my Christmas tree."

That same snow made the Dolphins want to go back home to sunny southern Florida and sit under a palm tree. Because it wasn't the first time Miami had been victimized by bad weather in Foxboro. On another December day twenty-two years earlier, New England and Miami played one of the most memorable games ever played by the Patriots anywhere, in any weather conditions.

It was criminal, then-Dolphins coach Don Shula insisted, what Patriots coach Ron Meyer did in sending a plow on to the field to clear a spot in the ice and snow for Pats kicker John Smith to boot what would turn out to be the game-winning field goal in a 3–0 victory for New England. And that was before Shula learned that the plow was driven by a convict on work-release from Walpole State Prison, Mark Henderson.

It was December 12, 1982, and the two long-time AFC East rivals were in the fourth quarter of a scoreless tie. Both teams were having trouble moving the ball. Passing was next to impossible, with winds gusting up to 30 miles per hour, the fingers of quarterbacks and receivers as cold as icicles, and the ball like a frozen rock. So both offenses kept the ball on the ground. It was 3 yards and, instead of a cloud of dust, a flurry of snow. Actually, 3 yards was one of the longer gains, as the linemen in the trenches looked like snowbound cars, spinning their wheels, unable to gain enough traction to move forward.

Players on both teams, and on both sides of the ball, were slipping and sliding throughout the frigid afternoon. New England's only scoring opportunity had gone awry late in the second quarter when Smith, attempting what normally would have been an easy chip shot from 18 yards, slipped on the snowy field and kicked the ball off the helmet of one of his linemen.

So, when the Patriots finally got another chance, reaching Miami's 16 yard line with just 4:45 remaining in the game, they weren't going to take any chances. New England called a time-out, and Smith dropped to his knees and began to scrape at the snow, trying desperately to clear a spot from which to kick. But his efforts quickly were interrupted by the roar of a tractor coming his way.

Waved on to the field by Meyer, Henderson swept along the 20 yard line, then suddenly veered over to where Smith and his holder Matt Cavanaugh were trying to clear the ground. "I was just trying to find a spot to put the ball down," Cavanaugh said. "The next thing I know, the tractor was coming up behind me. I

Convict Mark Henderson and his controversial plowing antics helped the Patriots defeat the Miami Dolphins on December 12, 1982. AP/Wide World

didn't know what to make of it. He must have seen me mark off a spot before the time-out, because he drove right over the middle of where I was going to put the ball down."

Meyer at first denied he had signaled to Henderson to go on to the field, even though he had been spotted running along the sideline, waving frantically. "I was just waving at the kicker to kick it through," he insisted. But, with the smile of a small boy caught with his hand in the cookie jar, Meyer finally had to admit to the truth. "I waved him on," Meyer at last acknowledged. "I wanted him to brush off the snow."

Shula certainly wasn't smiling. He was livid. Although it was cold outside, he was boiling hot under the collar. "It's hard for me to think," he said indignantly, "that anyone would take pride in doing that. I believe there's a rule in the book dealing with unfair

The Snowin' Samoan

It was as incongruous as a Laplander making his fortune by selling suntan oil in the West Indies, but Mosiula "Mosi" Tatupu, born under the palms of Pago Pago, American Samoa, and raised on the beaches of Honolulu, Hawaii, who played his college football in sun-drenched Southern California, was as at home in the ice and snow as any Eskimo.

A fan favorite for his congenial nature and exciting play on special teams, Tatupu didn't often get to the carry the ball for the Patriots. Except in the snow, when the 6', 227-pound fullback would crunch steadily forward, like a plow.

Tatupu earned the nickname "The Snowin' Samoan"—a variation of the moniker of Cincinnati quarterback Jack Thompson, who was known as "The Throwin' Samoan"—after rushing for a career-high 128 yards on 21 carries in miserable conditions in Foxboro against the Saints in December 1983.

Patriots center Pete Brock said that tackling Tatupu was like "trying to knock over a bowling ball with legs." Tatupu scattered Saints tacklers like tenpins that day. With his low center of gravity and uncanny sense of balance, he powered through the New Orleans defense, heading relentlessly toward the goal line, like a St. Bernard lumbering through the snow to rescue an injured skier.

It wasn't the first time Tatupu displayed his talent for performing well in adverse conditions. In the famous "Snow Plow" game against Miami in 1982, he had rushed for 81 yards, 54 of those coming on the fourth-quarter drive that led to John Smith's game-winning field goal.

"Everybody in the place knew what we were going to do," Patriots quarterback Tony Eason said after the New Orleans game. "But Mosi reads blocks so well. He didn't miss a read all day." "I just read the holes," Tatupu said, "tried to keep my balance, and stay as low as possible. You can't make quick cuts when the footing isn't good. You take what you can get. I try to make one cut, then power forward and get the yards."

acts. The thing that disturbs me most is [Meyer] taking pride in what he did. This is the last thing you'd want to see in pro football. The officials never should have let it happen. The official nearest me said he didn't see the guy come out until it was too late."

Bob Frederic, who refereed the game, explained the "official" point of view: "The game officials had no control over something like that. At the time when the sweeper came out, it was not under our control or jurisdiction in any way."

Frederic added that, had the Dolphins been able to move into position for a game-tying field goal, he would have insisted that a spot be plowed for them, too. "We very clearly told Coach Shula that we would also have swept their area," he said. That was no consolation to Shula, who said Meyer would "have to live with" his decision.

Pangs of conscience seldom plagued Meyer, who had come to New England from Southern Methodist University, where he'd resurrected a moribund program by recruiting the likes of running backs Eric Dickerson and Craig James. "I went to bed and slept soundly," Meyer said. "I was elated with the victory. I think the whole incident was blown out of proportion.

"I was unaware of any illegal aspects. To me it was just a spur-of-the-moment decision. There wasn't anything malicious about it. I saw John on his hands and knees, trying to get the snow cleared, and, all of a sudden, it hit me: Why not send a plow out there? I kept looking for it, but I had trouble finding it. I was about to forget about the whole thing when I saw [Henderson], so I ran down and told him to plow the spot John was trying to clear."

The mark left in the snow by Henderson, who was serving a fifteen-year sentence for burglary, and his infamous plow also left an indelible mark on Patriots history.

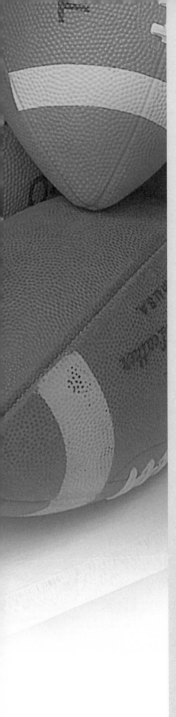

The Coach

I've got to fess up. Got to be honest. Got to come clean. I never thought Bill Belichick would turn out to be a great head coach. Or even an average one, for that matter. Just didn't see it ever happening. Not after what I'd seen in Cleveland, where he was reviled, rather than revered, after four losing seasons in five years in which he was remembered best—or, more accurately, worst—for tossing local hero Bernie Kosar out on his ear.

And certainly not after watching his rambling resignation speech as "HC of the NYJ"—the curt, and more than a little bizarre, phraseology he used in the hastily scrawled note he wrote to say he would not be succeeding his long-time mentor, Bill Parcells, as head coach of the New York Jets.

That was January 4, 2000, and Belichick on that day seemed much more like a reincarnation of Captain Queeg than the second coming of Vince Lombardi. All that was missing were the ball bearings. And, it appeared, perhaps a few of Belichick's marbles. Looking even more disheveled than usual, Belichick was dissembling, disingenuous, and disoriented during a rambling, voice-cracking, somewhat surreal, and certainly downright weird, press conference.

Just twenty-three days later, he was named coach of the New England Patriots. And just two years after that, he was holding the Lombardi Trophy over his head, having led the Patriots to a stunning upset of the heavily favored St. Louis Rams, who had come into the Louisiana Superdome billed as "The Greatest Show on Turf."

He's won two more championships since then, improving his postseason record to an all-time, NFL-best 10–1, just ahead of the legendary Lombardi's 9–1 mark with the Packers. "People thought I was nuts to give up a first-round pick for him," said Patriots owner Robert Kraft, who had to fork over New England's number-one draft choice in 2000 as compensation—or, if you will, ransom—for Belichick. "But I had gotten to know him when he was with us as the defensive coordinator. I thought he had one of the finest football minds I've ever encountered."

I admit it. I was one of those people who thought Kraft was out of his mind to hire Belichick. Give up a first-round draft

Bill Belichick has trans-
formed the Patriots into
champions. Joe Robbins

Border War

It was Bill Parcells who called it "the border war." As regional rivalries go, it didn't begin to compare in length or intensity with the nearly century-long feud between the Red Sox and Yankees. But for the three years it lasted, from 1997 to 1999, the relationship between the Jets and Patriots was bitter and rancorous enough to rate comparisons with the Hatfields and McCoys.

It was Parcells who touched it off, bailing out of New England to return to New York, where he had made his reputation winning two Super Bowls with the Giants. But he wasn't going back to the Giants, which would have been understandable and, perhaps, even forgivable. Instead, he was going to take over as coach of the Jets, a division rival of the Pats since the founding of the old AFL. As if that weren't bad enough, the timing of the move was even worse.

The news that Parcells, who had returned the Patriots to respectability, would be returning to the Big Apple broke when the Pats were in the Big Easy—New Orleans—to take on the Packers in Super Bowl XXXI.

Anyone who knows Parcells knows how much he hates to lose, so there is no question that he did his best to prepare the Patriots to play in that game. Although given the circumstances, how good could his best have been? Obviously he could not devote his full attention to playing the Packers because of the rumors swirling regarding his intention to abscond to the Jets. And there's no question that such talk was a distraction to his team, which wound up losing to Green Bay 35–21.

At any rate there was acrimony and animosity, tumult and turmoil, bad blood, bad feelings, and bad words during the three years Parcells coached the Jets, who improved after his arrival, while the Patriots went into a decline, their record slipping in each successive season under Parcells's successor, Pete Carroll.

The two teams met twice a year in games that quickly became known as "Tuna Bowls" (Parcells's nickname is "The Big Tuna"). The Jets won four of six, including two of three in Foxboro. The antagonism between the teams was as obvious as that between "red" states and "blue" states, and Patriots owner Robert Kraft clearly was in a disgruntled state whenever he thought of Parcells.

The two didn't speak for years, until January of 2000, when they had to negotiate the terms by which Bill Belichick would be allowed to get out of his contract to coach the Jets and come to New England to coach the Patriots. It was Parcells who broke the silence.

"I told [Kraft] it was Darth Vader calling," Parcells said. "He said he knew who that was. We had a chance to talk amiably. We had a few laughs about things that had happened in the past, some things I think we're both sorry happened. There are a few things I did wish I could do over again. That's life. He was a new owner. I was an older coach. Sometimes that's hard. Probably now he would, with his experience, understand me a lot better, and I certainly would understand him a lot better."

One of the things Parcells didn't understand when he was coaching in New England was why Kraft had him "cook the meals" but didn't let him "shop for the groceries"—which is to say that Parcells wanted control over personnel. That was just one of the many disagreements between the new owner and the highly successful coach with the large ego.

Parcells had stepped down as coach of the Giants because of health concerns after winning his second Super Bowl in the 1990 season. He was lured back to the sidelines in 1993 by James Orthwein, who was seeking to restore credibility and respectability to the Patriots after purchasing the team from Victor Kiam.

The Pats picked Drew Bledsoe with first choice overall in the 1993 draft, and Parcells started the kid at quarterback on opening day. The team, which had been 2–14 the previous year (and 1–15 in 1990) lost

(continued)

ten of its first eleven games under Parcells but finished with a flourish, winning its final four. The improvement continued the following year, when the Patriots won their final seven games of the regular season, qualifying as a wild card team for the playoffs, where they were beaten in the opening round in Cleveland by Belichick's Browns. After taking a step backward in 1995, when they slipped to 6–10, Parcells led the Patriots to only the second Super Bowl in team history in 1996, when they won the division title for the first time since 1986.

With a talented, young quarterback and a brilliant and charismatic coach, everything seemed on the upswing for the franchise—until Parcells blindsided Kraft by jumping to the Jets.

There were plenty of people who thought Parcells had taken advantage of Kraft yet again when he pried a first-round draft choice out of the Pats in 2000 in exchange for allowing Belichick to come to New England. As it turned out, it was the deal that paved the way for the Patriots to become the NFL's best team, while Parcells since has moved on to Dallas, where he struggled to return the Cowboys to their former glory.

choice? I wouldn't have given a plugged nickel for Belichick's chances of winning the Super Bowl.

Hey, it wasn't as if he'd been a rousing success in Cleveland, where he was disliked not only by many of his players, but also by many of the people in the Browns organization, and just about everybody in the media. His drafts weren't very good, and neither was his record: 36–44 from 1991 through 1995.

There were jokes in Cleveland about how the dour Belichick was the first man to successfully undergo charisma-bypass surgery, and how if he happened to be in a bar during Happy Hour, he'd be asked to leave lest he spoil the mood.

But it was Belichick and the Patriots who wound up having the last laugh, and a trio of Super Bowl trophies, too.

The contrast between his first five seasons in New England and those five long years in Cleveland is stunning. With the Patriots, Belichick has firmly established a reputation as the best coach in the business, a brilliant tactician who, working in conjunction with vice president for player personnel Scott Pioli—who had been a scout in Cleveland during Belichick's tenure and also is the son-in-law of Bill Parcells—has built a highly successful, remarkably consistent team.

Before Belichick's first Super Bowl, when the Patriots pulled off their stunning 20–17 upset of the Rams, veteran defensive end Anthony Pleasant, who had played for Belichick in Cleveland, then with the Jets, and, finally, New England, talked about the differences he noticed. "When he left Cleveland," Pleasant said, "I didn't think he'd get another job as a head coach. There was so much negative publicity around what happened there, I thought it would be hard for another owner to hire him.

"He did some things that didn't go over very well in Cleveland. He didn't listen to anybody. He didn't relate to the players. It was always, 'This is the way we did it in New York, and this is the way we're doing it here.' He's not like that any more. He's not a know-it-all with a chip on his shoulder like he was with the Browns.

"He's not the same person. After what I saw in Cleveland, I hesitated to come to the Patriots. Before I did I spoke with some guys here who were in Cleveland. Every one of them told me that he wasn't the same guy and had learned from his mistakes."

It's an assessment with which Belichick readily agrees. "I've learned a lot since 1991," he said. "A lot on the field, and a lot off the field. I think I'm more flexible now."

Pleasant wasn't the only one who doubted if Belichick, after what happened in Cleveland, would ever again be a head coach in the NFL. "I didn't know if I'd get another chance," Belichick said.

But he knew that if he did, he do some things differently. As coach of the Browns, he had a tendency to micromanage. "I'm kind of a detail-oriented person," Belichick said, "and I probably had a tendency to do too much. I've definitely delegated more in New England."

Which is not to say that Belichick doesn't keep his keen eye on even the smallest detail that could affect the success of his team. "He is so thorough," said Dante Scarnecchia, who has had a remarkable tenure as assistant coach with the Patriots, working on the staffs of Ron Meyer, Raymond Berry, Dick MacPherson, Parcells, Pete Carroll, and now, Belichick. "Each morning, Bill will come into each meeting and say, 'Here are three or four things you need to touch on today.' Sometimes it involves something that he's seen in practice the day before. He always makes it clear what he wants, and he doesn't miss anything."

"He points out things," Pats quarterback Tom Brady says, "you'd never even think about."

Part of the reason for that is because, like a chess grand master, Belichick is thinking several moves ahead of everybody else in the game. "He always seems to be at least two steps ahead," said Charlie Weis, who left his job as offensive coordinator in New England after the 2004 season to become head coach at Notre Dame.

Offensive coordinator Charlie Weis discusses strategy with quarterback Tom Brady.
AP/Wide World

"It's not just Xs and Os," Weis said. "It's personnel. It's the whole organization. He's thinking ahead, rather than just staying on an even keel. I think that gives him a decisive edge over most people he's going against. There are a lot of people who are good at Xs and Os. But there are very few people who have the insight, the foresight, to look ahead and try to figure out what to do before situations even come up."

Brilliant as the defensive coordinator for Parcells with the Giants, Patriots, and Jets, Belichick now is frequently referred to as a "genius" as a head coach. "I don't know about him being a genius," Weis said with a laugh. "I'd have to check his IQ. I do know this: No matter who he's playing, his players seem to know what the other team is doing before they do it. Now, that's not by accident, okay? They have a plan. They know what to do. He obviously has a clue. If that qualifies as genius, that definition, then it fits."

A misfit in Cleveland, Belichick has proven to be the perfect fit in New England, where, of all his many astute moves, none stands out more than his decision to keep Brady as his quarterback, rather than Drew Bledsoe.

But first, a little history.

In Cleveland in 1993, Belichick made the wildly unpopular—at least among Browns fans—decision to replace the much-beloved Kosar with Vinny Testaverde. What made it even worse was that Testaverde was hurt at the time Belichick pulled the trigger, which meant Todd Philcox had to step in for a while. "That," Pleasant recalled, "is when the fans went against him."

No matter that Testaverde led the Browns to an 11–5 record, plus a playoff victory over Parcells's Patriots, the following year. The populace had soured on Belichick, and things turned truly nasty in 1995, after team owner Art Modell announced he would be moving the Browns to Baltimore.

Fast forward now to the 2001 season. Bledsoe, who had been the first player taken in the 1993 draft, had recently signed a ten-year contract worth $103 million. Under Parcells he'd taken the Patriots to the playoffs in 1994, and to the AFC championship in

1996. He was a favorite of the Kraft family and of many Patriots fans, as well. There were few people in New England, when the 2001 season started, who doubted that the future of the franchise was in Bledsoe's hands.

Belichick, however, was increasingly impressed by Brady, who hadn't been taken until the sixth round in 2000, the 199th pick overall. When Bledsoe was hospitalized with a sheared blood vessel in his lung following a devastating hit by Jets linebacker Mo Lewis in the second game of the season, Belichick installed Brady as the starter, over veteran backup Damon Huard.

But that wasn't the daring move, the insightful move, the move that, more than any other, showed Belichick's brilliance — and guts — and turned the Patriots into champions. That came two months later, when Bledsoe had returned to health and was ready to play.

The Patriots had just fallen to 5–5 following a Sunday night loss to the Rams in Foxboro in which Brady had thrown two interceptions. The Saints were coming to town the following week, and Bledsoe wanted his job back. It was at that point that Belichick announced he was sticking with Brady. "Drew hasn't been able to play the last eight weeks," Belichick explained at the time. "Tom's more game-ready. That's the way we're going to go."

Although he was 5–3 as a starter, Brady hadn't looked all that sharp against the Rams. But, as it turned out, the St. Louis game would be the last the Patriots would lose that season. With Brady at quarterback, the Patriots won their last six regular-season games, then beat Oakland and Pittsburgh to win the AFC championship before stunning St. Louis in Super Bowl XXXVI.

"This isn't about Drew losing a job or being beat out," Belichick said in announcing what was a controversial decision. "It's strictly about the team. I can't control what other people think. All I can do is get the team ready. I would hope that everybody would respect the time, effort, and energy that I take in getting the team ready to play at its highest level."

They most certainly do now. Belichick has earned the respect of just about everyone who follows the NFL—particularly those who, like myself, never thought he'd turn out to be a great coach. And a great leader.

Time magazine even went so far, in April 2004, as to include Belichick in its annual list of the "100 most powerful and influential people in the world." Amusingly, the headline under his picture was: "Not as Dull as He Seems." *Time* further stated: "He's so unhip, he's cool."

"He's not as dull as people think," Phil Simms, the former Giants quarterback who's now a broadcaster for CBS, told *Time*. "Heck, he goes to Bon Jovi concerts! I once told Bill I had a video of him dancing at one of those concerts. He had this frightened look in his eyes."

That's the look opposing quarterbacks have when they have to play against a Belichick-designed defense. Creative and innovative, daring and detailed, when it comes to drawing up a defensive game plan, Belichick is the best in the game today. That's never changed.

But the coach has. Why, he even shows a dry sense of humor now. "This isn't my second job," he says of his highly successful stint in New England. "It's my fifth. I was coach of the Jets three times, for a total of nine days."

Coaching History

Bill Belichick has more wins (sixty through 2004) and a higher winning percentage (.682) than any other head coach in Patriots history. Here's a complete list of the men who have been at the helm since the club's inception in 1960:

Name	Years	Record	Percentage
Lou Saban	1960–61	7–12–0	.368
Mike Holovak	1961–68	53–47–9	.528
Clive Rush	1969–70	5–16–0	.238
John Mazur	1970–72	9–21–0	.300
Phil Bengtson	1972	1–4–0	.200
Chuck Fairbanks	1973–78	46–41–0	.529
Hank Bullough-Ron Erhardt	1978	0–1–0	.000
Ron Erhardt	1979–81	21–27–0	.438
Ron Meyer	1982–84	18–16–0	.529
Raymond Berry	1984–89	51–41–0	.554
Rod Rust	1990	1–15–0	.063
Dick MacPherson	1991–92	8–24–0	.250
Bill Parcells	1993–96	34–34–0	.500
Pete Carroll	1997–99	28–23–0	.549
Bill Belichick	2000–04	60–28–0	.682

Note. Saban was released after five games in 1961; Rush was released after seven games in 1970; Mazur was released after nine games in 1972; Bullough and Erhardt served as co-coaches for the final game of the 1978 season; Meyer was released after five games in 1984.

Tom Terrific

He is a Celebrity, with a capital C.

See Tom Brady shaking hands with the president at the White House. See Tom Brady kissing the pope's ring at the Vatican. See him out on the town with Hollywood starlet Bridget Moynihan. Or, before her, Tara Reid. See Tom hobnobbing with Hugh Hefner at the Playboy Mansion. See him hanging with Mickey Mouse at Disney

World. See him pictured on a Wheaties box. See him . . . well, you get the picture, don't you?

Did I say picture? He's as photogenic as they come, with his dimpled chin—usually covered with a scruffy-but-stylish day's growth of beard, a brilliant smile that flashes across his handsome face even more quickly than he can find an open receiver, and all-around, all-American-boy good looks on a 6'4", 225-pound frame.

No wonder Tom Brady's a certified, genuine Star, with a capital S.

See him throwing out the first ball at a Red Sox game in Fenway Park. See him knocking a golf ball around at Pebble Beach in the AT&T Celebrity Pro-Am. He has, by the way, a 7 handicap, and you just know he'd be a scratch player if he devoted the time to golf that he does to football.

Ah yes, football. That is, after all, what Tom Brady does best. So see him, too, with a couple of most valuable player awards after leading the Patriots to a trio of Super Bowl victories. Which means, of course, that you've also seen him on the covers of countless sports publications.

But here's the thing you might not have seen about Tom Brady. Even though he could have a lifestyle that would make the legendary Broadway Joe Namath seem like a monk, he's a regular guy. "What makes him special," Patriots owner Robert Kraft says, "is that he isn't caught up in his own celebrity."

Even though Brady is a celebrity, he doesn't act like one. And he certainly doesn't think of himself as one. He's one of the guys in the locker room, where his teammates respect and appreciate him but certainly don't hold him in awe. They frequently make him the butt of jokes, and Brady laughs as hard as anyone. "He's

Tom Brady led the Patriots
to three Super Bowl
victories in four years.
Joe Robbins

not an arrogant guy," tight end Christian Fauria said. "He doesn't think he's better than us. He's everyone's buddy."

Everybody likes Tom Brady. As Fauria says, "Men want to be him and women want to be with him."

What's not to like? "There's hardly anything you can criticize the guy for," said Patriots coach Bill Belichick. "He works hard. He treats every teammate with respect. He doesn't expect anything than everyone else doesn't get, too." "He's a reflection," Kraft said, "of his parents and the value system they taught him."

Brady is the youngest of four children of Tom and Galynn Brady, and the only boy. Growing up in San Mateo, just south of San Francisco, young Tommy—as family members still call him—had as his earliest athletic motivation the goal of emerging from the considerable shadow cast by his talented older sisters. As a kid he was known as "Maureen Brady's little brother," and it certainly kept him humble to hear people wonder if his arm would ever be as good as that of his oldest sister, who was an All-America softball pitcher at Fresno State, where she had a career earned run average of 0.98.

At Junipero Serra High—alma mater of the likes of Steelers all-time great wide receiver Lynn Swann—Brady showed enough promise as a catcher to be drafted in the eighteenth round by the Montreal Expos, who would have taken him higher except that he had let it be known he was going to go to Michigan to play football.

"Football is very important to me," Brady says now. "But it's not the only thing in my life. It's something I do. It's not who I am. My life ultimately is about the relationships I have with my family and my friends.

On Second Thought . . .

Six quarterbacks were selected ahead of New England's Tom Brady in the 2000 NFL draft:

Player	Team	Round	Pick	College
Chad Pennington	N.Y. Jets	1	18	Marshall
Giovanni Carmazzi	San Francisco	3	65	Hofstra
Chris Redman	Baltimore	3	75	Louisville
Tee Martin	Pittsburgh	5	163	Tennessee
Marc Bulger	New Orleans	6	168	West Virginia
Spergon Wynn	Cleveland	6	183	Southwest Texas State
Tom Brady	New England	6	199	Michigan

"My parents raised me in a way that I'm always thankful for what other people are doing. One thing you realize when you play a team sport is that everybody, not just one guy, is responsible for any success you may have. I don't think I've ever lost sight of that. Nor do I think I ever will. The reasons we've been successful in New England are because of a lot of sacrifice, a lot of hard work, by a lot of people. It's certainly not a one-man band. I feel lucky to be a part of it."

The Patriots are at least a little bit lucky to have him, since he was still available in the sixth round of the 2000 draft, after 199 players, including six quarterbacks, already had been taken. Brady had been hoping he'd be drafted by the 49ers, the hometown team he'd grown up rooting for, back in the days when his father had season tickets for the games at Candlestick Park.

"That's when I realized I wanted to be a football player, going to all those games growing up," he said. "I loved the 49ers. I'd gone to a whole bunch of their games. I had posters of Joe Montana and Jerry Rice on my walls. I remember sitting in my living room as the 49ers were drafting that day and seeing them pick a quarterback in the third round. I was so mad."

Anger would be just one of the emotions felt now by San Francisco fans, who wound up with Hofstra quarterback Giovanni Carmazzi when they could have had Brady. "A lot of teams took quarterbacks that year," Brady recalled. "Cleveland took a quarterback [Spergon Wynn]. San Francisco took a quarterback. The Jets took [Chad] Pennington; Pittsburgh took Tee Martin. The Saints took [Marc] Bulger. I was the 199th pick. I'll never forget that day."

The 49ers undoubtedly would rather not remember passing on Brady, whose passing has drawn comparisons with the great Montana. And with NFL record-holders Dan Marino and Peyton Manning, too.

Just as Montana and Marino always were being measured against each other, so, too, are Brady and Manning. What is strikingly similar is that Manning, like Marino, puts up better numbers and generally is considered a better "pure passer." But, while Manning, like Marino, gets the records, it is Brady who, like Montana, gets the championship rings. "Individual stuff has never meant a lot to me," Brady said. "I'm excited when we win games."

That's readily apparent to his teammates and opponents alike. "The most obvious thing about him—and the best thing about him—is that he wins," said Pittsburgh safety Troy Polamalu, whose Steelers lost to Brady and the Pats for the second time in four years (with both defeats coming at Pittsburgh's Heinz Field) in the 2004 AFC Championship Game.

"We've got a quarterback," kicker Adam Vinatieri said moments after the Patriots had followed up that win in Pittsburgh by beating the Eagles in Super Bowl XXXIX, "who's more concerned about wins than stats and being a self-promoting guy. You can talk about the stats, and all this, and all that, but I'd take this guy any day of the week. He just impresses me every week. He does things every week that are unbelievable."

Brady's success in the NFL has been no surprise to his college coach, Lloyd Carr. "He was one of the greatest leaders I've ever been around," Carr said. "Tom Brady is a poster boy for perseverance, determination, and commitment. He has poise and confidence that are special. You'll never see him panic. He has a special knack and ability to operate at his very best under the greatest conditions of pressure."

Pressure doesn't seem to bother Brady. Like Montana, he plays his best in the biggest games. He's not the least bit arrogant, but he is clearly confident. Combining that confidence with the competence he displays in executing the Patriots complex passing attack inspires his teammates. He is calm, cool, efficient, and, as a result, highly effective.

He was much more nervous about his audience with Pope John Paul II in the summer of 2004 than he was about playing in front of a television audience of millions in his first Super Bowl. "It's the most nervous I've ever been meeting anyone in my life," Brady said of his visit to the Vatican. "I grew up a Catholic, so being able to visit and meet him is an experience I'll never forget. It was incredible."

So was Brady's performance in the final seconds of Super Bowl XXXVI, when, with John Madden saying the Patriots should sit on the ball and play for overtime, Brady brought his team from its own 17 yard line to the Rams 31. "The thought of taking a knee never crossed my mind," he said. "I was going to go out and win the game."

Belichick was thinking the same way. "We were going to get into our two-minute offense," the coach said, "and give it a shot. If we got the ball up the field, we'd stay with it. If Tom had gotten sacked or had a negative play, we certainly didn't want to give the ball back to the Rams. They were out of time-outs, so we felt we could run a couple of plays and, at the worst, have to run out the clock if we weren't able to pick up any yardage in the early part of the drive."

The big play, the one that set up Vinatieri's game-winning, 48-yard field goal as time expired, was a 23-yard pass to Troy Brown to the St. Louis 36 with 21 seconds remaining. "It's called 64-Max, All-In," Brady said. "Max means: 'Blockers, give me more time.' The receivers all run 'in' routes. The way the Rams play, they really read the quarterback's eyes. I was looking hard to the right, and Troy was able to slide in underneath. They lost sight of him, I hit him, and he did the rest."

What was even more remarkable was that Brady found time to rest before the opening kickoff. Arriving early at the Super-dome, he took a nap in the locker room. "I was laying on the floor and just fell asleep," he said. "When I woke up, I didn't think that I would feel as good as I felt. I'd kept telling myself all week that it was just another game, that it would just come down to playing good football."

Tom Brady rides with Mickey Mouse after the Patriots victory in Super Bowl XXXVI.
AP/Wide World

Brady constantly strives to be a better football player. The morning after he won his first Super Bowl, he said: "There are a lot of things I have to be better with, such as certain routes, certain drops, how to escape better in the pocket, how to avoid the rush and continue to look downfield. There's never going to be complacency with me. I'm looking for the next challenge. I'm going to enjoy this one for a little bit and then it's on to something better—like another ring."

Three years later, he had not just another championship ring, but two more.

"You always think, 'I'd be so nervous in the Super Bowl.' But that's when I feel best," Brady said after the Patriots beat the Panthers in Super Bowl XXXVIII, "because I feel like I'm most prepared. We practiced on Carolina for two straight weeks, and we were really prepared and ready to go. The nerves come from not knowing what to do. If you're confident going out there that you know what you're going to do, and you know what they're going to do, that's when you feel best. That's the way I felt going into that game against Carolina."

Thorough preparation is an important part of Brady's success. "Tom is a very hard worker," Belichick said. "He's a smart kid, and he's got a lot of confidence and natural leadership. He's not the most athletic quarterback in the league. He's no Michael Vick. But he has good field vision. He makes good decisions. He can see the defense, what they're doing, and can sort it out in a hurry."

Brady's passion for preparedness was strong as ever in the week leading up to New England's win over the Eagles in Super Bowl XXXIX in Jacksonville. "Most guys," Patriots safety Rodney Harrison said several days before that game, "are out having dinner, hanging out, and enjoying themselves. Guess where Tom was? He was in his hotel room by 10:00 P.M. It just shows his level of preparation and his level of thinking. He's such a smart guy. He's so grounded. As much success as he's had, to stay so level-headed is tremendous."

Patriots offensive coordinator Charlie Weis kiddingly complained during Super Bowl week—make that only half-kiddingly—that Brady was getting to be "a pain in the butt, really," constantly calling him up and asking questions or requesting Weis come to his room to go over something in the game plan they'd already covered in meetings. "He kept asking, 'Can we add this? Can we drop this?' I finally said to him, 'Can you give me a break and let me get some sleep?'" Weis said.

Brady wasn't about to let the Eagles catch him napping. "I've spent a lot of time honing in on what exactly we want to do," he said. "I've been over and over the game plan with our quarterbacks coach, Josh McDaniels, and our offensive coordinator [Weis], and Coach Belichick. I know exactly what we want to do and what to expect. I feel I know what needs to be done to counter what the Eagles will do defensively."

Then he went out and did it, improving his career postseason record to 9–0.

One of the reasons Brady may have focused so intensely on preparing for Philadelphia is that it kept his mind off the death of his grandmother, who passed away early in Super Bowl week. "She had been very ill for quite some time," he said. "She was ninety-four years old and lived a long and full life. It was kind of a situation where, in the last week or two, things took a turn for the worse.

"We were really, really close. She lived about a mile away. She had a swimming pool, so my sisters and I would go over there and use the pool. She was a great woman. It's been tough for her to get around, so she couldn't come to my games, but she always watched them. She'd have Super Bowl parties at her nursing home. She'd sit right in front of the TV, and we'd always get phone calls from her after the game.

"Any time a family member passes away, it's real tough. My mind has been here, but my heart has been at home. I wish I was there, but duty calls here. It's part of the commitment I have to this team. A lot of people deal with issues in their life, and you just have to put it in one part of your mind. You can't really let it dis-

Twice as Nice

When quarterback Tom Brady was named the most valuable player of
the Patriots 32–29 victory over Carolina in Super Bowl XXXVIII to close
the 2003 season, he joined a select group of only four men to earn
the award more than once (Brady also won it in Super Bowl XXXVI).
San Francisco quarterback Joe Montana is the only man to win the
award three times, while Green Bay quarterback Bart Starr and Pittsburgh quarterback Terry Bradshaw were two-time winners. Here is a
complete list of Super Bowl most valuable players through 2005:

Super Bowl	MVP	Team
I	QB Bart Starr	Green Bay
II	QB Bart Starr	Green Bay
III	QB Joe Namath	N.Y. Jets
IV	QB Len Dawson	Kansas City
V	LB Chuck Howley	Dallas
VI	QB Roger Staubach	Dallas
VII	S Jake Scott	Miami
VIII	RB Larry Csonka	Miami
IX	RB Franco Harris	Pittsburgh
X	WR Lynn Swann	Pittsburgh
XI	WR Fred Biletnikoff	Oakland
XII	DT Randy White and DE Harvey Martin	Dallas
XIII	QB Terry Bradshaw	Pittsburgh
XIV	QB Terry Bradshaw	Pittsburgh
XV	QB Jim Plunkett	Oakland
XVI	QB Joe Montana	San Francisco

Super Bowl	MVP	Team
XVII	RB John Riggins	Washington
XVIII	RB Marcus Allen	L.A. Raiders
XIX	QB Joe Montana	San Francisco
XX	DE Richard Dent	Chicago
XXI	QB Phil Simms	N.Y. Giants
XXII	QB Doug Williams	Washington
XXIII	WR Jerry Rice	San Francisco
XXIV	QB Joe Montana	San Francisco
XXV	RB Ottis Anderson	N.Y. Giants
XXVI	QB Mark Rypien	Washington
XXVII	QB Troy Aikman	Dallas
XXVIII	RB Emmitt Smith	Dallas
XXIX	QB Steve Young	San Francisco
XXX	CB Larry Brown	Dallas
XXXI	KR-PR Desmond Howard	Green Bay
XXXII	RB Terrell Davis	Denver
XXXIII	QB John Elway	Denver
XXXIV	QB Kurt Warner	St. Louis
XXXV	LB Ray Lewis	Baltimore
XXXVI	QB Tom Brady	New England
XXXVII	S Dexter Jackson	Tampa Bay
XXXVIII	QB Tom Brady	New England
XXXIX	WR Deion Branch	New England

Tom Brady celebrates the Patriots victory over the Carolina Panthers in Super Bowl XXXVIII. AP/Wide World

tract you a whole lot and allow it to take away from your preparation. When it's time to play football, you have to go play football."

That's when Brady's at his best.

"You can tell he's out there to win games," Pats running back Patrick Pass said. "You can see it in his eyes, and you can hear it in his voice. He wants to win." "He makes great decisions," veteran wide receiver Troy Brown said of Brady. "That's what it really comes down to—not making bad throws, throwing into bad coverages.

"He's been a great leader. He works hard in the weight room, works hard in the film room. He really shows guys how it's supposed to be done. What really makes him special is how he stays cool under pressure. He's been able to make big plays in key situations. When you can make those plays, you win big games."

You also become a Celebrity.

"I don't know how I would deal with that sort of stuff," said Dan Koppen, the Patriots center. "Tom goes through so much that we don't know about. It's got to become a pain to him after a while. But he's been able to grow and handle situations that the normal person isn't capable of handling."

Having gone quickly from NFL obscurity to fame, Brady knows how quickly things could turn around if he didn't keep his priorities in order. "I realize how fast it all came," he said, "and how fast it can all go. I know I can't take any shortcuts in how I work or prepare. I'm not that good."

Oh, but he is. He is Tom Terrific, almost too good to be true. He is a true Celebrity, with a capital C. Except, of course, in the locker room, where he's just one of the guys. And at home with his family, where he's still Tommy.

Dynasty

Tom Brady evaded the question as if it was a pass rusher, sensing it coming, and adjusting his position just enough to let it go harmlessly past. "You guys all want me to say it," Brady said after the Patriots won their second straight Super Bowl, and third in the last four years, to close the 2004 NFL season. "But I'm not going to say it."

What everyone was trying to get Brady to say, in those euphoric moments after New

England defeated the Eagles, 24–21, at Alltel Stadium in Jacksonville in Super Bowl XXXIX, was that with that victory the Patriots had established themselves as a modern-day dynasty.

But as far as the Patriots are concerned, *dynasty* is a four-letter word. "We never really self-proclaim ourselves anything," Brady said. "That's not our style. We just love playing ball. We have a great coach. We have a great owner. And we have a great time playing together. We've tried to express to people what this team is all about. We really are a team. I mean, in four seasons, I've never had a receiver complain about not getting the ball. I've never had a running back complain about not getting enough carries. I have an offensive line that always busts their butts every day. And we have a defense that's just unreal. For us, it's not so much about we've accomplished in the grand scheme of things. You take one at a time and realize how tough they are."

Only one other team in NFL history has won three Super Bowls in a span of just four years—the Dallas Cowboys of 1992, 1993, and 1995. The Patriots, by matching that feat, unquestionably have established themselves as the twenty-first century's first "Team of the Decade." What the Cowboys were to the 1990s, the 49ers to the '80s, the Steelers to the '70s, and the Packers to the '60s, the Patriots have become in the present day.

Whether New England has established itself as a dynasty, however, is an entirely different question, the answer to which hinges on an entirely different definition of "dynasty."

Times and teams certainly change, and so do terms. There is no argument about which are the truly great sports dynasties. There were the Yankees of 1949 through 1964, when they won fourteen pennants and nine World Series—including five in a

Corey Dillon brought new life to the Patriots running game in 2004.
Joe Robbins

row from 1949 through 1953. The Boston Celtics won eleven NBA titles in thirteen years, from 1957 through 1969, including eight straight from 1959 to 1966. In the NHL (you remember the NHL, don't you?) the Montreal Canadiens won the Stanley Cup six times in eight years from 1953 through 1960—five in a row from 1956 to 1960—and were beaten in the finals the other two years. They'd also lost in the finals in both 1951 and 1952. Then, between 1965 and 1979, the Canadiens won ten more titles.

Now those were dynasties.

It does not in any way detract from the amazing achievements of those teams to point out that they were accomplished under vastly difference circumstances than now exist in professional sports. There was no free agency in baseball during the glory days of the Yankees, nor was there a draft. Teams could sign as many young players as they could afford, and those players were bound to the team in perpetuity.

Montreal, for many years, was annually awarded its choice of any junior hockey player of French-Canadian descent, which led to such names as Jean Beliveau, Maurice Richard, Bernard Geoffrion, Jacques Plante, and Guy Lafleur appearing so often on Lord Stanley's Cup. And, don't forget, there were only six teams in the league until 1967.

As for the Celtics, it was the genius of Red Auerbach, who acquired Bill Russell and Bob Cousy, and the lack of a salary cap, that enabled the Celtics to become pro basketball's greatest dynasty. In the NFL the advent of free agency and a firm salary cap have made it impossible to retain the type of talent stockpiled by the Packers, Steelers, and even the 49ers.

Are the Patriots a dynasty the way those teams were? No, not yet. Probably not ever, given the economic realities of today's NFL and the greater number of teams dividing the talent pool. They are, however, a modern-day dynasty. That doesn't mean standards have slipped—only that they've had to be adjusted as times have changed. In the old days of pro sports, three championships in four years would have qualified a team as a very good one but not one of the all-time greats; not yet a dynasty. In today's sports world, however, three championships in four years—especially in pro football, where there are so many injuries and the talent is spread so thin—is a record of dynastic proportions.

"I don't know," said safety Rodney Harrison, when asked after beating the Eagles if the Patriots were a dynasty. "I just know that we won this game, and we're champions. I will leave that up to all you experts. I mean, you get paid to figure those things out. I just get paid to play. I'm just going to sit back and enjoy this."

It truly has been a joy to watch the Patriots in recent years. Their win over the Eagles made it thirty-two in thirty-four games, a streak that included a league-record twenty-one in a row, counting three postseason victories early in 2004.

But what they've done is not as impressive as how they've done it. In an era filled with selfish players who worry more about their own salary and statistics than their team's record, the Patriots have been an anomaly. "We play as a unit," defensive back Asante Samuel said. "We understand that there is no 'I' in team. We work hard. We do everything that we are supposed to do."

That may sound more than a bit corny, but it is absolutely true. The Patriots have become the "53 musketeers"—one for all, all for one. It started in 2001, the year they won their first Super

Ty Law runs for a touchdown after intercepting a pass in Super Bowl XXXVI.
AP/Wide World

Bowl. It was then that, instead of being introduced individually before games, the Patriots decided they would come out together, as a team. It was a small gesture, but it became a symbol of how, once the opening whistle blew, they would play the game. There have been many teams over the last four years who have sent more players to the Pro Bowl than the Patriots. But no team has won nearly as many titles.

In assessing the team's string of successes, veteran wide receiver—and, in 2004, part-time defensive back—Troy Brown said, "This is how you play the game."

If there is one game that best exemplifies how the Patriots play as a team, it would not be any of their Super Bowl victories, nor any of their other playoff wins. It would, in fact, be a game that only Patriots fans likely will remember.

The game in which the Patriots really showed us something—actually, the game in which the Patriots showed us a little bit of everything—was against the Rams in St. Louis the first Sunday in November 2004. That was the game in which the Pats showed us a kicker throwing a touchdown pass—off a fake field goal—to a wide receiver who had spent much of the afternoon playing defensive back.

That was the game in which the Patriots also showed us heart. They showed us a linebacker making a highlight-film catch in the end zone for a touchdown. They showed us character and ingenuity, creativity, adaptability, and resiliency, as well.

They showed how, with both starting cornerbacks sidelined by injuries and then another going down on the first pass thrown by the Rams, they could adjust and limit one of the NFL's most wide-open offenses to just 2 touchdowns. Only the week before, in a rare defeat in Pittsburgh that put an end to their record-setting winning streak, the Patriots had lost All-Pro corner Ty Law for what would prove to be the remainder of the season. (He was released by the team after the Super Bowl.) Earlier in the year, veteran corner Tyrone Poole had suffered a season-ending injury. And when Samuel, a 185-pounder, hurt his shoulder tackling the Rams 288-pound tight end, Brandon Manumale-una, the New England secondary appeared to be in a desperation situation against one of the NFL's most prolific passing offenses.

On the corners for New England were Randall Gay, an undrafted rookie agent, and Earthwind Moreland, who had been signed off the practice squad the previous week. Seeing action at safety were rookie Dexter Reid, a fourth-round draft choice, and Don Davis, a thirty-one-year-old journeyman line-backer. Davis wasn't the only player switching positions. Brown, in his twelfth year in the league, made his first appearance as a defensive back, a position he would continue to play the rest of the year.

"Anybody on this team would have done it," Brown said of having to play not only on offense and defense, but also on special teams, returning punts. "It was a need that had to be filled for the team, and I was able to step up to the challenge and do it." That's what the Patriots have done whenever they've faced a challenge. Despite playing with a patchwork secondary, they routed the Rams 40–22.

"The Rams throw the ball very well," Pats coach Bill Belichick said proudly. "They have a great group of receivers. But Earthwind and Gay and Troy went out there and battled. That's

Young fans cheer during the Super Bowl victory parade in Boston on February 8, 2005. *AP/Wide World*

what this team is all about—being prepared to step up when called upon. There were so many guys who stepped up, who came through for us and made big plays. It was probably as complete a team victory as I've ever been around."

Among the big plays was a diving catch for a touchdown by linebacker Mike Vrabel, playing tight end for New England in goal-line situations. Brown also had a touchdown catch, but not from Brady. Instead it came from kicker Adam Vinatieri, when the Rams were caught napping while lining up for what they thought was going to be a field-goal attempt by the Patriots.

"I'm really proud of our football team," Belichick said.

Super Patriots

Here are the box scores from the three Super Bowls that the Patriots have won under the direction of head coach Bill Belichick through 2005:

SUPER BOWL XXXVI

February 3, 2002 · Louisiana Superdome, New Orleans, Louisiana

St. Louis	3	0	0	14	–	17
New England	0	14	3	3	–	20

StL—FG Wilkins 50

NE—Law 47 interception return (Vinatieri kick)

NE—Patten 8 pass from Brady (Vinatieri kick)

NE—FG Vinatieri 37

StL—Warner 2 run (Wilkins kick)

StL—Proehl 26 pass from Warner (Wilkins kick)

NE—FG Vinatieri 48

Attendance—72,922

Team Statistics	St. Louis	New England
First downs	26	15
Rushing yards	90	133
Passing yards	337	134
Total yards	427	267

SUPER BOWL XXXVIII

February 1, 2004 · Reliant Stadium, Houston, Texas

Carolina	0	10	0	19	–	29
New England	0	14	0	18	–	32

NE—Branch 5 pass from Brady (Vinatieri kick)

Car—Smith 39 pass from Delhomme (Kasay kick)

NE—Givens 5 pass from Brady (Vinatieri kick)

Car—FG Kasay 50

NE—Smith 2 run (Vinatieri kick)
Car—Foster 33 run (pass failed)
Car—Muhammad 85 pass from Delhomme (pass failed)
NE—Vrabel 1 pass from Brady (K. Faulk run)
Car—Proehl 12 pass from Delhomme (Kasay kick)
NE—FG Vinatieri 41
Attendance—71,525

Team Statistics	Carolina	New England
First downs	17	29
Rushing yards	92	127
Passing yards	295	354
Total yards	387	481

SUPER BOWL XXXIX
February 6, 2005 · ALLTEL Stadium, Jacksonville, Florida

New England	0	7	7	10	—	24
Philadelphia	0	7	7	7	—	21

Phil—Smith 6 pass from McNabb (Akers kick)
NE—Givens 4 pass from Brady (Vinatieri kick)
NE—Vrabel 2 pass from Brady (Vinatieri kick)
Phil—Westbrook 10 pass from McNabb (Akers kick)
NE—Dillon 2 run (Vinatieri kick)
NE—FG Vinatieri 22
Phil—Lewis 30 pass from McNabb (Akers kick)
Attendance—78,125

Team Statistics	New England	Philadelphia
First downs	21	24
Rushing yards	112	45
Passing yards	219	324
Total yards	331	369

The Patriots are a proud team, but not an arrogant nor a boastful one. Other teams talk trash. The Patriots let their play do the talking. There is no better example of that than Brady, who is undefeated in nine postseason games, the winner of three Super Bowls in four years as a starter. "Tom symbolizes this team," veteran linebacker Roman Phifer said, "with the way he carries himself. He understands that no one guy can win the Super Bowl by himself. That's the attitude most of the guys have here. We don't have ego problems. We're able to pull together and get a lot more accomplished by playing as a team.

"If Tom wasn't the way he is, it probably could affect us. That's when egos come in, and guys start maybe to question what's more important—their own self-gratification or the team? All those things can be a cancer that can gut a team from the inside and cause it to fall apart. But we have great character guys. They're not about to let that happen."

How good, Belichick was asked after Super Bowl XXXIX, is this Patriots team? "I'll leave the comparisons and historical perspectives to everybody else," he said. This from a man who now is being compared with the legendary Vince Lombardi following a win over Philadelphia that upped his postseason record to 10–1, which surpasses the 9–1 mark Lombardi compiled with the Green Bay Packers.

Vrabel was asked, after New England's latest Super Bowl victory, where he thought the Patriots deserved to rank in NFL history. "That's a really good question," he said. "I don't really know. But I'd have to say that we're not necessarily done. Our goal is to win championships. As long as we're playing, we'll try to win them. I don't think we're necessarily finished."